Football for Kids (Ages 8-12)

Engaging stories, fun quizzes and trivia designed to teach life skills, boost confidence, and inspire young athletes to be role models on and off the field

Blitz Books

© **Copyright Blitz Books 2025 - All rights reserved.**

The content within this book may not be reproduced, duplicated or transmitted without direct written permission from the author or the publisher.

Under no circumstances will any blame or legal responsibility be held against the publisher, or author, for any damages, reparation, or monetary loss due to the information contained within this book. Either directly or indirectly. You are responsible for your own choices, actions, and results.

Legal Notice:

This book is copyright protected. This book is only for personal use. You cannot amend, distribute, sell, use, quote or paraphrase any part, of the content within this book, without the consent of the author or publisher.

Disclaimer Notice:

Please note the information contained within this document is for educational and entertainment purposes only. All effort has been expended to present accurate, up-to-date, and reliable, complete information. No warranties of any kind are declared or implied. Readers acknowledge that the author is not engaging in the rendering of legal, financial, medical or professional advice. The content within this book has been derived from various sources. Please consult a licensed professional before attempting any techniques outlined in this book.

By reading this document, the reader agrees that under no circumstances is the author responsible for any losses, direct or indirect, which are incurred as a result of the use of the information contained within this document, including, but not limited to, — errors, omissions, or inaccuracies.

Book Cover by Blitz Books
Illustrations by Blitz Books

1st edition 2025

Contents

Introduction — VI

1. The Basics of Football — 1
    1.1 Football's Beginnings
    1.2 Beginning the Game
    1.3 Scoring Points: Touchdowns, Field Goals, and Safeties
    1.4 Plays
    1.5 Player Positions Explained: Who Does What?
    1.6 Football Equipment: What Do Players Wear?
    1.7 Understanding the Game: Time, Overtime and Officials
    1.8 The Football Field

2. Football Skills and Techniques — 19
    2.1 Passing Like a Pro: Techniques Quarterbacks Use
    2.2 Catching Basics: Improving Hand-Eye Coordination
    2.3 Running with the Ball: Tips from Top Running Backs
    2.4 Defensive Moves: Learning to Tackle Safely
    2.5 Kicking and Punting: Mastering Special Teams Skills
    2.6 Strategies and Plays: Thinking Like a Coach

3. Legendary Players and Their Journeys — 33
    3.1 Walter Payton: More Than Just Rushing Yards
    3.2 The Story of Jerry Rice: Dedication Leads to Success
    3.3 Sarah Fuller: Breaking Barriers in Football
    3.4 More Women in Football: Expanding the Game
    3.5 Overcoming Challenges: Lessons from Doug Flutie

  3.6 Lesser-Known Heroes: Players Who Made a Difference
  3.7 Young Talents in NFL History: Prodigies of the Sport
  3.8 More Football Legends: Humble Start to Greatness

4. Football, Fitness, and Health   47
  4.1 Training Routines of Top Football Players
  4.2 Eating Right: Nutrition Tips for Young Athletes
  4.3 Staying Active: Exercises for Off-Season Training
  4.4 The Importance of Mental Health in Sports
  4.5 Handling Injuries: Prevention and Care
  4.6 Balancing School and Sports: Tips for Student-Athletes

5. Values Learned Through Football   59
  5.1 Teamwork
  5.2 Trust
  5.3 Communication
  5.4 Leadership Skills Every Young Athlete Can Develop
  5.5 Fair Play: Learning Sportsmanship Early
  5.6 Overcoming Challenges: What Football Teaches Us About Resilience
  5.7 Setting Goals and Achieving Them Through Sports
  5.8 The Role of Discipline in Football Success
  5.9 Learning from Mistakes: Feedback on the Field

6. Making Football Fun   73
  6.1 Football Trivia: Fun Facts and Quizzes
  6.2 What Would You Do? Scenario-Based Questions
  6.3 Football in Movies and Books: Pop Culture Fun
  6.4 Hosting a Football Themed Party

7. Football for All: Diversity and Inclusion   83
  7.1 Breaking Stereotypes: Diverse Backgrounds in Football
  7.2 Accessibility in Sports: Making Football Inclusive
  7.3 From All Walks of Life: Unique Football Stories

  7.4 Charities and Causes Supported by Football Players
  7.5 The Role of Fans: Supporting Your Local Team
8. Beyond the Game   95
  8.1 From the Field to the Classroom: Applying Football Discipline to Academics
  8.2 Leadership Skills on and off the Field
  8.3 Football and Community Service: Giving Back
  8.4 Future Careers in Football Beyond Playing
  8.5 Football and Education: Learning Beyond the Field

Conclusion   107

References   111

Introduction

Hey there!

Alright, let's talk football. Not the kind with the black and white round ball and endless running (though that's cool too), but the kind with helmets, touchdowns, and some serious teamwork. If you're between the ages of 8 and 12, and you've ever felt the rush of catching a football or cheering for your favorite team from the stands or your couch, this book is for you.

Football isn't just a game; it's a whole world of excitement, strategy, and teamwork. Imagine being part of a team where every player has a role to play, and every move can change the game. Whether you're throwing a perfect spiral, making a game-saving tackle, or cheering from the sidelines, football teaches you about working together, sticking with it when things get tough, and celebrating victories, big and small.

Before we get to that though, let me tell you a little about myself. I believe in the magic of sports for kids. I've always thought of football as more than just a weekend activity; it was a way to learn important life lessons and bring people together. My goal with this book is to share my passion and help you become a better person and perhaps if you play…a better player.

So this book is about football—how to throw, catch, and understand the game. But it's more than that. Think of it as a playbook for life. You'll find stories of famous players who started just like you, fun quizzes, and trivia to test your knowledge. We'll also dive into how football can boost your confidence, teach you about teamwork, and inspire you to be a role model, whether you're on the field or not.

Role models are super important. Players like Tom Brady, J. J. Watt, and even lesser-known heroes all have lessons to teach us. It's not just about their success, but the challenges they've overcome.

Did you know that Jerry Rice, one of the greatest receivers of all time, was told he was too slow to play in the NFL? He worked harder than anyone else to prove them wrong. These stories show how determination, hard work, and a positive attitude can get you through anything.

Football is for everyone, and that's something we'll celebrate throughout these pages. You'll read about incredible female athletes and players from all backgrounds. It's a sport that welcomes everyone.

By the end of this book, you'll know all about the basics of the game, from what a touchdown is to how to throw a perfect pass. You'll also learn about the amazing athletes who play the game and the science behind those jaw-dropping plays. We'll talk about what you need to eat to stay strong and healthy and how to keep your head in the game even when things get tough.

Get ready to learn, be inspired, and have a blast. Football has so much to teach us, and I'm excited to share that with you. So grab your favorite snack, find a comfy spot, and let's get started on this adventure together.

Dream big, work hard, and believe in yourself. Welcome to the world of football—let's make it an unforgettable journey!

Let's go!

Chapter 1

THE BASICS OF FOOTBALL

Have you ever watched a football game and felt the excitement build as the quarterback threw a perfect pass, or the thrill of a player sprinting down the field to score a touchdown? This chapter will help you understand what makes football so amazing and why it's loved by millions of people. We'll explore the basics, from its origins to the rules, positions on the field, and the equipment players wear.

1.1 Football's Beginnings

American football is a game filled with action, strategy, and skill. The origins of football date back to the late 1800s when it evolved from two other sports: soccer (known as football in most parts of the world) and rugby. The first game of American football was played in 1869 between Rutgers and Princeton. The game was quite different back then, with fewer rules and more chaos on the field. Over the years, football has changed a lot, adding rules and regulations to make it the exciting and strategic game we know today.

soccer ball *rugby ball* *football*

While American football is most popular in the United States, its influence spreads worldwide. There are professional leagues in other countries, like the Canadian Football League (CFL) and several European leagues. The NFL even hosts games in England, Mexico, and Brazil to reach international fans. Though football isn't as globally popular as soccer, it's steadily gaining fans from around the globe. These international games help spread the love of football, showing that it's a sport for everyone, everywhere.

Football isn't just a game you watch on TV; it's a huge part of American culture. Think about the Super Bowl, the biggest football event of the year. Families and friends gather to watch the game, eat delicious snacks, and enjoy halftime shows. Whether it's a small-town high school game or a professional NFL game, football is a great way to spend time with your friends and family.

1.2 Beginning the Game

The game starts with the captains of each team meeting at mid-field with the officials. Each team picks their own captains and they can have one or many. An official flips a coin while the visiting team calls heads or tails. The team winning the **coin toss** picks if they want to be on offense or defense first. The other team picks which end of the field they want to defend. The teams line up on the field, and the kickoff starts the game. Let's go!

Each play begins with the offense lined up at the **line of scrimmage**. The team on offense has four **downs**, or tries, to get the ball ten yards down the field. If they do that, they get another four downs to try and again get ten more yards further. If they can't, they have the option to punt on 4th down to kick the ball as far down the field as possible for the other team to start on offense. If they're close enough though, they might have their kicker try a field goal. Their coach can also choose to try and get the remaining yards to achieve another first down. That's called **going for it**. You might notice the down markers on the side of the field which show everyone which down the current play is. Knowing the basics helps to understand the game!

Coin toss is just what it sounds like and includes the official and captains from each team.

The **line of scrimmage** is where the ball is placed for the start of a play. It changes as the players move the ball on the field.

The numbered **down** is the number of tries, 1-4, the offense can have to get ten yards further down field.

Going for it is a term that teams use on 4th down when they leave their offense on the field to try to get the remaining yards needed for a first down.

1.3 Scoring Points: Touchdowns, Field Goals, and Safeties

Scoring points in football gets everyone on their feet, cheering and high-fiving. There are several ways to put points on the board, and each method has its own excitement and strategy. Let's start with the most thrilling of all: the touchdown. A **touchdown** is worth six points and happens when a player carries the ball into the opponent's **end zone**. Imagine the roar of the crowd as a wide receiver leaps to catch the ball, landing safely in the end zone with defenders hot on their heels. After scoring a touchdown, the team gets a chance to earn extra points. They can kick the ball through the **uprights** for one extra point from the 15 yard line, known as the **extra point** or **PAT** (Point After Touchdown). Or they can attempt a **two-point conversion** by running or passing the ball into the end zone again from the two-yard line, adding a bit more drama and risk.

Another way to score is by kicking a **field goal**, which is worth three points. Field goals are usually attempted when the team is close to the end zone but not close enough to try for a touchdown, or when time is running out and they need some quick points. The kicker steps up, aiming to send the ball sailing through the goalposts. It's a moment that requires precision and nerves of steel, especially in high-pressure situations. For instance, think of the last few seconds of a tied game, the kicker lines up, the crowd holds its breath, and the ball splits the uprights—three points on the board and the win!

Then there's the **safety**, a rare but exciting way to score that's worth two points. A safety occurs when the defense tackles an offensive player with the ball in their own end zone. A safety can also be called when an offensive player commits a penalty in their own end zone. It's a big momentum shift because not only does the defense score two points, but they also get the ball back right after. Imagine the surprise and excitement as the defense fights to break through the offensive line, finally bringing the ball carrier down in the end zone. The scoreboard changes, and the crowd goes wild. It's a moment that's unexpected and exhilarating, adding a unique twist to the game.

> A **touchdown** (6 points) happens when a player runs into their opponent's end zone with the ball or catches it there.
>
> **End zones** are the two areas on each end of the football field that are ten yards deep. They are usually decorated in the teams colors.
>
> **Goal posts** are at the very end of both sides of the field, past the end zones, yellow and are made up of the uprights and the crossbar.
>
> **Uprights** are the vertical posts of the goal post. They are 35 feet tall and 18.5 feet apart.

Crossbar is the horizontal bar of the goal post. It's ten feet off the ground.

Extra point or PAT (point after touchdown) is the point added after the TD if the kicker makes the kick through the uprights.

The **two-point conversion** is two more points (instead of one extra point) added after a TD if the offense takes the ball into the end zone on one try after lining up at the two yard line.

A **field goal** is worth three points, usually kicked on 4th down, when the offense is farther away from the end zone.

A **safety** is a score by the defense if they tackle an offensive player in their own end zone. Also, if the offense receives a penalty while in their own end zone, a safety will be called.

1.4 Plays

When it comes to game strategies, teams use a mix of offensive and defensive plays to gain an advantage. On offense, teams might use a running game, where the quarterback hands the ball off to a running back who tries to advance it down the field. This strategy is great for controlling the clock and wearing down the defense. Alternatively, teams might opt for a passing game, where the quarterback throws the ball to a wide receiver or tight end. This can result in big yardage gains quickly but comes with the risk of incomplete passes and interceptions. Most teams use combinations of these offensive plays on a regular basis. On defense, strategies can vary widely. Some teams focus on stopping the run by crowding the line of scrimmage with big, strong players to tackle the running back. Others might prioritize defending against the pass by positioning fast, agile players in the secondary (further back from the line of scrimmage) to cover receivers and intercept passes. **Blitz**ing is another defensive strategy where additional players rush the quarterback, hoping to sack him before he can throw the ball or hand it off. Each team has its own playbook filled with a variety of plays and strategies, and the key to success often lies in choosing the right plays at the right times.

Football history is filled with iconic games that have left fans talking for years. One such game is the "Ice Bowl" of 1967, where the Green Bay Packers faced the Dallas Cowboys in the NFL Championship Game. Played in brutally cold conditions, with temperatures plunging to -13 degrees Fahrenheit, the game ended in a dramatic last-minute **quarterback sneak** by Bart Starr, giving the Packers the win. Another unforgettable game is Super Bowl LI (51), where the New England Patriots made a historic comeback against the Atlanta Falcons. Down 28-3 in the third quarter, the Patriots rallied to win 34-28 in overtime, the first Super Bowl ever to go into overtime. These games are memorable not just for the scores but for the incredible displays of skill, determination, and heart.

To make sure you've got a good grasp of how scoring works in football, let's do a quick quiz. Grab a pencil and see how many you can get right!

Quiz Section

1. **How many points is a touchdown worth?**
A) 3 points
B) 6 points
C) 1 point

2. **What is an extra point and how many points is it worth?**
A) A kick through the goalposts, worth 1 point
B) A run into the end zone, worth 2 points
C) A field goal, worth 3 points

3. **What is a safety and how many points does it score?**
A) When the offense scores in their own end zone, worth 1 point
B) When the defense tackles an offensive player in their own end zone, worth 2 points
C) When the defense intercepts the ball, worth 3 points

4. **What is a two-point conversion?**
A) A field goal by the kicker
B) A run or pass into the end zone after a touchdown
C) An interception

5. **How many points is a field goal worth?**
A) 6 points
B) 2 points
C) 3 points

6. **What kinds of plays do most teams run?**
A) Pass plays
B) Run plays
C) Combination of pass and run plays

I hope you enjoyed learning about the different ways to score points in football. Each method brings its own excitement and strategy to the game, making it one of the most thrilling sports to play and watch.

> A **blitz** is when additional defenders come through the line of scrimmage to get to the QB or disrupt the play.
>
> **Quarterback sneak** is when the QB fakes a handoff to a RB, but keeps the ball instead to try to sneak forward a few yards.

Answers: 1B, 2A, 3B, 4B, 5C, 6C

1.5 Player Positions Explained: Who Does What?

Football is like a well-oiled machine, where every player has a specific role that contributes to the team's success. The whole goal for the offense is to score points. Let's break down who does what on the field, starting with the **offensive positions**. The **quarterback**, often called the QB, is the leader of the offense. Think of the QB as the brains of the operation, making split-second decisions and throwing passes to move the ball down the field. A famous quarterback you might know is Matthew Stafford, who's known for his great passing ability. The **running back** is another key offensive player. This player's main job is to run with the football after getting handed the ball by the quarterback. They need to be fast and agile, like Christian McCaffrey or Ezekiel Elliott, who dodge defenders with ease. Then, there's the **wide receiver**. This player catches passes from the quarterback and needs to be quick on their feet and have great hands. Mike Evans is a great example and has over 1,000 yards receiving in his first ten years in the league. **Tight ends** are similar to wide receivers as they too catch passes but they also help the offensive line players by blocking. Travis Kelce is a strong blocker as well as being able to catch the ball in the midst of being tackled. **Offensive line** is a group name for the **center**, **guards** (right guard and left guard), and **tackles** (right tackle and left tackle) who line up at the line of scrimmage. The center hikes the ball to the QB and then they help the guards and tackles block the other team from getting to their QB or disrupting the play.

Offensive players:

- Quarterback
- Running back
- Wide receiver
- Tight end

Offensive line:

- Center
- Guards
- Tackles

Now, let's switch gears to the **defensive positions**. The main goal of the defense is to stop the offense from scoring. Lining up at the line of scrimmage is the defensive line. If there is a player lined up across from the center on offense, it is the **nose tackle**. Defense also has **guards** and **tackles** but depending on the plan, their number changes. **Linebackers** are the versatile players of the defense. They need to be strong and fast because they tackle running backs, cover receivers, and sometimes blitz the quarterback. They can start behind the defensive line or at the line. T.J. Watt is a defensive player famous for his fast moves and leadership on the field. **Cornerbacks** are the players who cover the wide receivers. They need to be quick and have great instincts to prevent the receiver from catching the ball. Someone like Jalen Ramsey, who is fast and has a knack for intercepting passes, is a great example. **Safeties** are the last line of defense. They help cover receivers and also support the linebackers in stopping the run. Ed Reed, a safety known for his ability to read the quarterback and make game-changing interceptions, is one of the best to ever play the position.

Defensive players:

- Nose tackle
- Guards
- Tackles
- Linebackers
- Cornerbacks
- Safeties

Then there are **special teams**. This is a crucial but sometimes overlooked part of the game. Special teams players come onto the field during kicking plays. They each have very important jobs to enable the kicker to make a good kick. The **kicker's** job is to kick field goals and extra points. They need to be precise, as their kicks can often decide the outcome of a game. Instead of a center hiking the ball, teams use a **long snapper** as they have further to hike the ball. The **holder**, typically the team's punter (but not always) receives the ball from the long snapper and places the football on the ground and holds it for the kicker. Adam Vinatieri is a kicker who has made some of the most memorable kicks in NFL history. The **punter** kicks the ball downfield when the offense can't get a first down and is forced to turn the ball over to the other team. There is no holder for a punt, but the punter receives the ball from the long snapper. A good punt can pin the other team deep in their own territory, giving the defense a better chance to stop them. Shane Lechler is a punter known for his powerful and accurate kicks.

Special teams positions:

- Place kicker
- Long snapper
- Holder
- Punter

To help you remember who does what, let's play a little matching game. Match each position with its role or a famous player from the list below. You'll see how each player fits into the bigger picture of the game.

Here's how it works: I'll give you a list of positions, roles, and famous players. Your job is to match them correctly.

Ready? Here we go!

Matching Games:

1. Quarterback (QB)
2. Running Back (RB)
3. Wide Receiver (WR)
4. Linebacker (LB)
5. Cornerback (CB)
6. Safety (S)
7. Kicker (K)
8. Punter (P)

A) Covers wide receivers
B) Last line of defense, supports run and pass coverage
C) Kicks field goals and extra points
D) Punts the ball downfield
E) Throws passes and leads the offense
F) Runs with the ball
G) Catches passes
H) Tackles running backs and covers receivers

---

1. Matthew Stafford
2. Christian McCaffrey
3. Mike Evans
4. T.J. Watt
5. Jalen Ramsey
6. Ed Reed
7. Adam Vinatieri
8. Shane Lechler

A) Linebacker
B) Safety
C) Punter
D) Quarterback
E) Wide Receiver
F) Kicker
G) Running Back
H) Cornerback

While you're matching them, think about what each player is known for and how they contribute to their team. This game will give you a better idea of how each position works and why every role is important.

> **Answers:** 1E, 2F, 3G, 4H, 5A, 6B, 7C, 8D
> 1D, 2G, 3E, 4A, 5H, 6B, 7F, 8C

1.6 Football Equipment: What Do Players Wear?

When you step onto a football field, you'll notice players look a bit like armored warriors. That's because they wear a lot of protective gear to keep them safe while they play. Let's start with the basics. The **helmet** is perhaps the most important piece of equipment. It's designed to protect players from head injuries like concussions. Modern helmets are made from hard plastic with a thick padding inside. They also have a face mask to shield the player's face from impact. Imagine riding a bike without a helmet—risky, right? Now, imagine charging into another player at full speed without one. That's why helmets are non-negotiable in football.

Next up are the **shoulder pads.** These pads are worn under the jersey and cover the shoulders, chest, and upper back. They're designed to absorb and distribute the force of impact when players collide. Think of shoulder pads like the airbags in a car; they cushion the blow to keep you safe. They might look bulky, but they're essential for protecting players from serious injuries. Along with shoulder pads, players wear padded pants to protect their thighs and knees. These pants have pockets for inserting pads that shield the lower body from impact.

Cleats are another crucial piece of gear. These are special shoes with spikes on the bottom to provide traction on the field. Whether the ground is muddy, wet, or dry, cleats help players run, pivot, and stop without slipping. Imagine trying to play football in regular sneakers—you'd likely be sliding all over the place. Cleats come in various styles, and players choose them based on the field conditions and their position. A player will have more than one set of cleats, as the length of the spike will change depending on the field condition.

Now let's talk about **jerseys and pants.** Players wear jerseys with their team's colors, and each jersey has a number that identifies the player.

Sometimes, you'll also see the player's name on the back. The numbers aren't just for show. They help referees, coaches, and fans keep track of who's who on the field. For example, quarterbacks usually wear numbers between 1 and 19, while wide receivers might wear numbers in the 80s. The uniform not only represents the team but also helps everyone understand the roles and responsibilities of each player.

In addition to the essential gear, many players opt for optional gear to enhance their performance and protection. **Gloves** are common among wide receivers and running backs. These gloves have sticky palms that help players grip the ball better, especially in wet or cold conditions. **Eye shields** or **visors** are another piece of optional equipment. These are clear or tinted shields attached to the helmet's face mask to protect the eyes from glare, dirt, and impact. Most players also wear **mouthguards** to protect their teeth and reduce the risk of concussions. The choice of optional gear often depends on the player's position and personal preferences.

Safety standards are a big deal in football. All equipment must meet specific regulations to ensure it provides adequate protection. Helmets, for example, undergo rigorous testing to make sure they can withstand significant impact. Players and coaches also regularly inspect gear to ensure it's in good condition. Wearing damaged or old equipment can be just as dangerous as not wearing any. Maintenance is key—just like you'd take care of a bike to make sure it's safe to ride, football gear needs regular checks and care.

In football, the right equipment can make all the difference. It's not just about looking cool; it's about staying safe and playing your best. So next time you watch a game, take a moment to appreciate the gear that keeps players protected while they give it their all on the field.

1.7 Understanding the Game: Time, Overtime and Officials

Watching a football game can sometimes feel like trying to solve a giant puzzle, but once you get the hang of it, it's like seeing the pieces fall perfectly into place. Let's break down the structure of a typical game to make it easier to follow.

A football game is divided into **four quarters**, each lasting 15 minutes. The clock stops frequently for reasons like incomplete passes or when a player runs out of bounds, which makes the actual time that the game lasts much longer. After the first two quarters, there's a break called **halftime**. Halftime is not just for players to rest and strategize; it's also when you get to sometimes enjoy entertaining performances and grab some snacks. The game resumes with the third quarter, followed by the fourth.

If the score is tied at the end of these four quarters, the game goes into **overtime**. Recently, the NFL has changed the rules for overtime. Overtime starts with a coin flip to determine who gets the ball first, just like the beginning of the game. If the team on offense first scores a touchdown, the game is over and they win. If they score a field goal or don't score at all, the other team gets the chance to possess the ball. If the second team also scores, then whoever scores next, wins. If they don't, then the team that scored already in OT is the winner. Now in the playoffs, overtime rules are a bit different. Both teams are guaranteed to have the ball at least once, no matter what. If the team that gets the ball first scores a touchdown, the other team still gets a chance to get the ball and try to score, too. If both teams score a touchdown, the game then goes into what's called **sudden death**, meaning whoever scores next, wins. But if the first team only scores a field goal or doesn't score at all, the other team has a chance to win by scoring more than the first team.

This new OT rule makes overtime more exciting and gives both teams an equal opportunity to win the game!

Now, let's talk about the role of **officials**. You might have seen referees on the field wearing striped shirts and wondered what they're up to. These officials are responsible for ensuring the game is played fairly and according to the rules. They call penalties, signal touchdowns, and keep an eye on the clock. Each official has a specific role. The **referee** is the head official and is responsible for the overall conduct of the game. This is the official that announces the penalties on the field to the fans. The **umpire** watches the line of scrimmage and focuses on the actions of the offensive and defensive lines. The **line judge** and **side judge** monitor the sidelines and ensure players don't step out of bounds. Officials use a series of hand signals to communicate their calls. For example, raising both arms straight up indicates a touchdown, while extending one arm forward with the other arm perpendicular to it signals a first down.

Understanding the flow of the game, along with the role of the officials, can make watching the game much more enjoyable because you'll know what's happening in real time. Knowing these elements helps you appreciate the beauty and complexity of the sport even more.

1.8 The Football Field

Imagine standing on a **football field**, the grass beneath your feet, and the giant expanse stretching out before you. A football field is a carefully measured rectangle, 120 yards long and 53.3 yards wide. The field is divided into two halves by the **fifty-yard line** right in the middle. Each half has markings every five yards, making it easy to see how far the ball needs to go. The **end zones**, located at either end of the field, are each 10 yards deep. These are the ultimate targets for offenses as that's where touchdowns are scored. End zones are often decorated with the home team's colors and logo, adding to the excitement of crossing into this sacred space.

Visualizing all these lines and zones can be a bit tricky, but think of it like a giant grid. The lines running across the field are called **yard lines**, and they help players, referees, and fans keep track of the ball's progress. The lines running the length of the field are known as **hash marks**, and they show where each play begins. There's also the **sideline**, marking the edge of the field, and the **goal line**, marking the start of the end zone. All of these lines are like a road map, guiding players as they strategize and move the ball.

To bring this all to life, imagine comparing a football field to other sports fields you might be familiar with. A soccer field, for instance, is larger—typically around 100 yards long but can stretch up to 130 yards. It's also wider, up to 100 yards. While a soccer field is open and less marked, a football field is densely packed with lines and zones, each with a specific purpose. Basketball courts, on the other hand, are much smaller—only about 94 feet long, and mainly focus on the key and three-point line. The football field's complexity, with its various zones and lines, makes it unique and much like a giant outdoor chess board where every move counts.

Creating a diagram of a football field can be helpful to understand the field and how it's laid out. Grab a large piece of paper and some markers, and draw the field with all its lines and zones. Label each part: the end zones, the fifty-yard line, the hash marks, and the sidelines. This hands-on activity will help you remember the field's layout and understand how it all fits together.

Remember, the field is a place where anything can happen. The next time you watch a game or play with friends, think about all the planning and effort that goes into every yard gained and every touchdown scored. Football isn't just a game of physical endurance; it's also a game of strategy and precision, much like the careful design of the field itself. So, as you learn more about the game, keep the image of that grid in your mind. It's the canvas where the incredible art of football unfolds.

Embrace the excitement, embrace the challenge, and most importantly, have fun exploring the wonderful world of football. As you continue to learn and grow on and off the field, remember that every great player started with a simple love for the game and a willingness to learn. Enjoy every moment, and let your passion for football guide you to new adventures and achievements.

Chapter 2
FOOTBALL SKILLS AND TECHNIQUES

Imagine this… You're on the football field, the crowd is roaring, and it's your time to shine as the quarterback. Or maybe you're watching your favorite team in an important game. The game is on the line, and everyone's counting on the quarterback to make the perfect throw. But how do you or they nail that pass like a pro? In this chapter, we'll break down everything you need to know about passing, from grip and stance to reading defenses and perfecting your throw. You can use this information whether you're playing with your friends and family for fun in your yard or playground or if you play on a school or recreation team. Understanding what the different position players practice and watch for during games helps us understand more about this game. So, grab a football, and let's get started!

2.1 Passing Like a Pro: Techniques Quarterbacks Use

First things first, let's talk about how to hold the football. A good grip is the foundation of a strong, accurate throw. When you hold the football, start with the laces up. Place your thumb under the football to provide support and your other four fingers on or by the laces. Play around with where it feels comfortable for your fingers to be that gives you the most comfort and control. You might want to have your index and middle fingers on the laces with the others just behind the laces. Or it might be more comfortable for you to have your middle three fingers on the laces. The ball should feel snug but not too tight in your hand. Stand with your feet shoulder width apart, knees slightly bent, and your weight balanced evenly. This stance gives you stability and helps you generate power when you throw.

Now, let's break down the mechanics of a good throw. A perfect pass starts with your body alignment. Your shoulders should be square to your target, and your throwing arm should come back, elbow bent at a 90-degree angle. As you begin to throw, step forward with your non-throwing foot, transferring your weight from your back foot to your front foot. This motion helps generate power. Your throwing arm should then come forward in a smooth, controlled motion, releasing the ball with a flick of your wrist. Your follow-through is important—your arm should continue moving forward, and your fingers should point toward your target. This ensures that the ball travels in a tight spiral, making it easier for your receiver to catch.

But passing isn't just about mechanics; it's also about strategy. Before the snap, quarterbacks need to read the defense to decide where to throw the ball. This involves looking at how the defensive players are lined up and predicting their movements. For example, if the cornerback is playing close to the receiver, it might indicate man-to-man coverage, meaning the cornerback will follow the receiver closely. If the cornerback is playing further back, it might be zone coverage, where the defense covers specific areas of the field. By understanding these cues, quarterbacks can make smarter decisions about where to throw the ball, increasing their chances of completing the pass.

Practice is essential to getting better at passing. One simple but effective drill is target practice. Set up a few targets at varying distances and practice hitting them with your throws. You can use small laundry baskets or hoops (or really anything) laid on the ground. Start with short passes and gradually work your way to longer throws. Another helpful drill is the drop back drill. Practice taking a few quick steps back from the line of scrimmage, then plant your feet and throw. This mimics what you'll do in a game and helps you get comfortable throwing on the move. Footwork drills are also crucial. Set up cones (or strings in a zigzag pattern) and practice moving through them quickly, keeping your eyes downfield. This helps improve your agility and balance.

Even the best quarterbacks make mistakes, but learning from them is vital. One common mistake is gripping the ball too tightly, which can affect your throw's accuracy. Remember to hold the ball snugly but relaxed. Another mistake is not stepping into the throw. Failing to transfer your weight can lead to weak, inaccurate passes. Always step forward with your non-throwing foot to generate power. Overthrowing and underthrowing are also common issues. To avoid these, focus on your follow-through and aim to release the ball at the right moment. Practicing regularly and paying attention to these details will help you improve over time.

Practice Drills Checklist
- Target Practice: Set up targets at different distances and practice hitting them.

- Drop Back Drill: Practice taking a few steps back from the line and then throwing.

- Footwork Drills: Use cones to practice moving quickly and maintain balance.

- Accuracy Drills: Focus on short, medium, and long throws to improve precision.

- Game Scenarios: Simulate game situations where you need to make quick decisions and accurate throws.

By focusing on these techniques and drills, you'll get better at being a passer. Remember, every great player started with the basics and built their skills through hard work and practice. So keep practicing, stay focused, and have fun!

2.2 Catching Basics: Improving Hand-Eye Coordination

Catching a football might look easy when you see pros doing it, but it takes practice and the proper technique. Wide receivers are the ones mostly catching passes, but running backs and tight ends do too. The first step is getting your hand positioning right. For an over the shoulder catch, when you're sprinting down the field and the quarterback throws a deep pass, you want to form a triangle with your thumbs and index fingers. This creates a secure pocket with which to catch the ball. For quick slants or fast passes, keep your hands open with your palms facing the ball and your fingers spread wide. Think of them like lobster claws, ready to snap shut on the ball. Your goal is to cushion the ball as it arrives, absorbing some of its speed to prevent it from bouncing off of your hands.

Hand-eye coordination is super important in catching. It's all about your brain telling your hands where to go and when. To get better at this, try some simple exercises. One great exercise is the tennis ball drill. Stand facing a wall. Throw a tennis ball against it, and then catch it with one hand. Switch hands and repeat. This helps you focus on tracking the ball with your eyes and reacting quickly with your hands. Another fun exercise is juggling. Start with two balls and work your way up to three. Juggling forces you to keep your eyes on multiple objects at once, improving your overall coordination.

Maintaining body control and balance can make all the difference when you're trying to catch a football, especially when you have to make those tricky midair adjustments. Imagine you're running full speed and need to jump to catch a high pass. Your ability to control your body in the air, twist, and land smoothly is crucial. Practice jumping and catching from different angles, and focus on landing on your feet. Balance exercises like standing on one foot or using a balance board can also help. These exercises strengthen your core muscles, which are key for maintaining stability both on the ground and in the air.

Catching drills are helpful to enhance your skills. One effective drill is the partner toss. Stand a few yards apart from a friend or family member and toss the ball back and forth. Start with short distances and gradually increase the distance as you get more comfortable. This drill helps improve your reaction time and catching accuracy. Another great drill is the fingertip push-up. Get into a push-up position (don't be afraid to start on your knees), but balance on your fingertips instead of your palms. This strengthens your fingers and hands, making it easier to grip and hold onto the ball. For a solo drill, try the tennis ball drill. Stand a few feet away from (preferably) an outside wall and throw the tennis ball against it, catching it as it bounces back. Another drill to try by yourself is to underhand toss a football high and in front of yourself, then taking a step or two and jumping to catch it. These can help you work on your hand-eye coordination and reaction time.

Catching Drills Checklist

- Partner Toss: Toss the ball back and forth with a friend, increasing distance gradually.

- Fingertip Push-Ups: Strengthen your fingers and hands by doing push-ups on your fingertips.

- Tennis Ball Drill: Throw a tennis ball against a wall and catch it with one hand to improve quick reactions.

- High Pass Catching: Practice jumping and catching high passes to improve body control and balance.

Now that you know the basics of catching, it's time to practice and see your skills improve. Keep working on your hand positioning, eye-hand coordination, and body control, and soon you'll be catching more balls.

2.3 Running with the Ball: Tips from Top Running Backs

When you're running with the ball, the last thing you want is to fumble and possibly have the other team recover it. That's why ball security is so important. Think of the football like a precious treasure that you need to protect at all costs. The best way to hold it is using the "high and tight" grip. Imagine you're cradling a baby chick. Hold the ball close to your chest, with your forearm wrapped around it and your fingers gripping it firmly. Your fingers should be holding the end of the football while your forearm protects the ball from defenders trying to knock it out. This grip keeps the ball secure, even when you're dodging and weaving through defenders. Practicing this hold during drills will make it second nature, ensuring you keep possession of the ball during those crucial moments in the game.

Being a successful running back isn't just about holding the ball; it's also about knowing where to go. This is where vision and awareness come into play. Great running backs have a knack for finding gaps in the defense, those tiny openings that let them burst through for big gains. To develop this skill, keep your eyes up and scan the field as you run. Look for the gaps your offensive line creates and anticipate where defenders might come from. Practicing with cone drills can help improve your field awareness. Set up cones to represent defenders and practice running through them, changing directions quickly. Over time, you'll get better at spotting those gaps and making quick decisions on the field.

Speed and agility are your best friends when you're carrying the ball. Being able to change direction quickly and outrun defenders can turn a small gain into a touchdown. Exercises like ladder drills are fantastic for improving agility. Lay a ladder flat on the ground (or simulate a ladder using string) and practice running through it, stepping in and out of each square as quickly as you can. This drill helps you develop quick feet and better control over your movements. Short sprints are another great exercise. Set up markers at different distances and practice sprinting between them, focusing on explosive starts and quick stops. These drills mimic the bursts of speed you'll need during a game, helping you become a faster, more agile player.

Blocking techniques are another crucial skill for running backs, as sometimes you'll need to protect yourself or help your teammates by blocking defenders. Effective blocking starts with a solid stance. Keep your feet shoulder width apart, knees bent, and hands ready. When you make contact with a defender, use your hands to push them away (not holding onto them in any way though) while keeping your body between them and the ball carrier. This requires strength and good technique. Practicing blocking drills with a partner can help you get better at this. Take turns being the defender and the blocker, focusing on using your hands and maintaining your balance. Good blocking can give your team the extra time needed to make a big play.

Running with the ball is an exhilarating part of football, filled with opportunities to make big plays and help your team win. By focusing on ball security, vision, agility, and blocking, you'll become a more effective and confident running back. Remember, every great player started with the basics and built their skills through practice and determination. So keep working hard, stay focused, and have fun out there!

2.4 Defensive Moves: Learning to Tackle Safely

Tackling in football is all about stopping the opposing player in their tracks; but safety is critical. When you tackle someone, the most important thing is to keep your head up. This means never leading with your helmet or face. Instead, focus on using your shoulders to make contact. Imagine you're giving someone a big bear hug but with a bit more force. Your head should be to the side of the player you're tackling, and your eyes should be up, looking at their waist or chest. This not only keeps you safe but also allows you to see what's happening and adjust if needed.

Positioning yourself correctly before you make a tackle can make all the difference. As a defensive player, you want to be in an athletic stance—feet shoulder width apart, knees bent, and weight balanced on the balls of your feet. This stance allows you to move quickly in any direction. When you're ready to tackle, aim to get low and drive up through your legs. The angle at which you approach the ball carrier is crucial. Coming in at a slight angle rather than head-on can help you avoid getting tackled. Think of it like trying to tag someone in a game of tag; you want to be close enough to touch them but not so close that they can easily slip by you.

One effective tackling technique is the "wrap and roll." This method is all about securing the opponent and bringing them down safely. When you make contact, wrap your arms around the player tightly, just like you're giving a big hug. Once you've wrapped them up, use your momentum to roll them to the ground. This not only stops their forward progress but also ensures they don't break free. The wrap and roll technique is great for bringing down players who are bigger or faster than you because it uses leverage and body control rather than just brute strength. Practice this technique with a partner, focusing on wrapping up tightly and rolling smoothly to the ground.

To get better at tackling, practice defensive drills that focus on both technique and reaction time. One simple drill is the tackle dummy drill. Here, you use a padded dummy to simulate a real opponent. Practice wrapping up the dummy and rolling it to the ground, focusing on keeping your head up and using your shoulders. Another great drill is the cone drill. Set up a series of cones in a zigzag pattern and practice moving through them quickly, simulating the movements you'll make during a game. This drill helps improve your footwork and agility, making you a more effective tackler. Reaction drills are also important. Have a partner act as the ball carrier and practice reacting to their movements. This helps you develop the quick reflexes needed to make successful tackles.

Defensive Drills Checklist

- Tackle Dummy Drill: Practice wrapping up a padded dummy and rolling it to the ground. Try wrapping up a couple of bed pillows with heavy-duty tape like duct tape and cover them with a pillowcase to make a padded dummy, if needed.

- Cone Drill: Set up cones in a zigzag pattern and practice moving through them quickly.

- Reaction Drill: Have a partner act as the ball carrier and practice reacting to their movements.

- Angle Drill: Practice approaching the ball carrier at different angles to improve your positioning.

Tackling is one of the most important skills in football, and learning to do it safely and effectively can make you a valuable player on the field. Understanding how players tackle also helps to understand the players we watch. By focusing on safe techniques, proper positioning, and practicing with drills, you'll become a strong and reliable tackler. Remember, every great defensive player started with the basics and worked hard to perfect their skills. So keep practicing, stay focused, and enjoy the thrill of making that perfect tackle.

2.5 Kicking and Punting: Mastering Special Teams Skills

When it comes to special teams, kicking and punting are two skills that can make a huge difference in a game. Let's start with the basics of kicking a football. Imagine you're about to kick the ball. Your body positioning is crucial. Stand a few steps back from the ball and a little to the side, depending on whether you're right or left-footed. As you approach the ball, take a few quick steps while keeping your eyes on the spot of the football where you want to make contact. Use the inside of your foot, right next to where your shoelaces are, to strike the lower half of the ball. This positioning helps you get the ball airborne and sends it straight through the goalposts. Your follow-through is essential, too; keep your leg swinging smoothly to guide the ball.

Now, let's talk about punting. Punting is different from placekicking because you're dropping the ball from your hands rather than kicking it off the ground. Hold the ball tilted horizontally with both hands, laces up, and take a few steps forward. As you drop the ball, your kicking leg should swing through in one smooth motion, striking the ball with the top of your foot. The goal is to get the ball high and far, giving your team time to get downfield and make a tackle. The drop is crucial; if you drop the ball too low or too high, it can mess up your kick. Practice dropping the ball consistently to develop a reliable punt.

Within special teams, every player has a specific role that contributes to the success of a kick or punt. The long snapper is responsible for snapping the ball accurately to the holder or punter. This snap needs to be quick and precise, as any delay can disrupt the timing of the kick. On the other hand, the holder catches the snap and places the ball on the ground for the kicker. Their job might seem simple, but it's incredibly important. They need to position the ball correctly and hold it steady so the kicker can make a clean strike. Then there are the blockers who protect the kicker from incoming defenders. Each role is vital, and a successful special teams play relies on everyone doing their job perfectly.

Improving your kicking and punting skills takes practice and consistency. One effective drill is to set up targets at different distances and practice hitting them. This helps you develop accuracy and control. Another good drill is to practice kicking or punting from various angles and positions on the field. This prepares you for real game situations where you might not always have a perfect setup. Consistency is key, so focus on making each kick or punt the same as the last. Working on your leg strength and flexibility can also help you generate more power and distance in your kicks.

Professional punters and kickers have their own unique styles and techniques, and studying them can provide valuable insights. For example, Chris Boswell, one of the most clutch kickers in NFL history, is known for his calm under pressure and precise technique. Watching videos of his kicks can show you how he approaches the ball and follows through. Another great example is Tommy Townsend, a punter known for his powerful and accurate punts. Analyzing how he drops the ball and the smoothness of his kicking motion can give you tips on improving your own punting technique.

Kicking and punting are more than just special teams skills; they're game-changers. A well-placed punt can pin the opposing team deep in their own territory, while a successful field goal can win the game. By focusing on the fundamentals, practicing regularly, and studying the pros, you can develop your kicking and punting skills to help your team succeed. Whether you're aiming for the goalposts or sending the ball soaring downfield, remember that every great kicker and punter started with the basics and built their skills through hard work and dedication. Keep practicing, stay focused, and enjoy the thrill of making that perfect kick or punt.

2.6 Strategies and Plays: Thinking Like a Coach

When you think of football, you might picture fast-paced action and big plays. But at the heart of it all is strategy, and that's where playbooks come in. A playbook is like a secret recipe that coaches and players use to plan their moves. Inside, you'll find a collection of plays the team might use during a game, each designed to outsmart the opponent. Imagine it as a treasure map guiding you to the end zone. Each play has specific routes for receivers, blocking schemes for linemen, and assignments for every player. Teams spend hours studying their playbooks so that when they hit the field, they know exactly what to do.

Let's break down a few basic offensive plays. One of the simplest is the run play. In a run play, the quarterback hands the ball off to a running back, who then tries to advance it down the field. This play is great for gaining short yardage and controlling the clock. Another common play is the pass. Here, the quarterback drops back and looks for an open receiver to throw the ball to. Pass plays can cover a lot of ground quickly but also come with the risk of interceptions. Then there's the option play, which combines elements of both running and passing. The quarterback starts the play as if it's a run but has the option to pass the ball if he sees an opportunity. This play keeps the defense guessing and can lead to big gains if executed well.

On the defensive side, formations are key to stopping the offense. One of the most popular defensive setups is the 4-3 defense. In this formation, there are four defensive linemen and three linebackers. The linemen's job is to pressure the quarterback and stop the run. At the same time, the linebackers cover the middle of the field, ready to tackle any ball carrier who gets past the line. The 4-3 defense is versatile and can adapt to various offensive plays. Another common formation is the 3-4 defense, which has three linemen and four linebackers. This setup puts more emphasis on the linebackers, who can either rush the quarterback or drop back into pass coverage. The 3-4 is great for confusing the offense and creating opportunities for turnovers.

Understanding game situations is crucial for making smart decisions on the field. Let's talk about third down, one of the most critical moments in any game. On third down, the offense has one last chance to gain the necessary yardage for a first down before they're forced to punt or attempt a field goal. Coaches often choose plays with a high chance of success, like short passes or runs designed to catch the defense off guard. Another important situation is the two-minute drill, which happens at the end of each half. During this time, the offense needs to move quickly to score before the clock runs out. This usually means more pass plays and quick passes to the sidelines to stop the clock. The goal is to manage the clock effectively while advancing the ball.

In football, every play and every decision counts. Knowing your playbook, understanding basic offensive and defensive plays, and being aware of game situations can give you the edge you need to succeed on the field. So, next time you watch a game or play with your friends, think about the strategies behind each move. Who knows? You might just be the player who helps lead their team to victory.

Chapter 3

LEGENDARY PLAYERS AND THEIR JOURNEYS

Picture this: You're on a football field, the crowd is cheering loudly, and you're about to be a part of a play that will be remembered for years. That's the kind of magic legendary players bring to the game. In this chapter, we'll dive into the stories of some of football's greatest heroes, starting with one of the most iconic running backs of all time—Walter Payton. His journey is filled with record-breaking achievements, inspiring community work, and a legacy that continues to influence the world of football today.

3.1 Walter Payton: More Than Just Rushing Yards

Walter Payton, often called "Sweetness" for his smooth playing style, is a name that echoes through the halls of football history. Imagine a player so good that he could glide past defenders with ease, making everything look effortless. That was Walter Payton. His career was nothing short of spectacular. With 16,726 rushing yards, Payton held the record for the most rushing yards in NFL history until Emmitt Smith broke it in 2002. His unique running style combined power, speed, and agility, making him nearly impossible to bring down. Payton wasn't just about running through defenses; he was also known for his incredible endurance and ability to play through pain, often carrying his team with how well he played.

But Walter Payton's greatness extended far beyond the football field. Off the field, he was a hero in his own right, dedicating much of his time and resources to helping others. One of his most notable contributions was the Walter Payton Cancer Fund, which he established after being diagnosed with a rare liver disease that ultimately took his life. Through this fund, he aimed to raise awareness and support for cancer research, helping countless individuals and families affected by the disease. Payton's commitment to community service didn't stop there. He was actively involved in various charitable activities, always looking for ways to give back and make a difference. Whether it was visiting sick children in hospitals or supporting local youth programs, Payton's impact on his community was profound.

Walter Payton's legacy continues to inspire both on and off the field. His incredible achievements and contributions were recognized in various ways, but perhaps the most significant honor was the renaming of the NFL Man of the Year Award to the Walter Payton NFL Man of the Year Award. This prestigious award is given every year to an NFL player who excels not only in their performance on the field but also in their community service. It's a fitting tribute to a man who showed what it means to be a role model and a leader. Payton's influence can still be felt today as players strive to follow in his footsteps, balancing athletic excellence with a commitment to making the world a better place.

Reflection Section: What Would You Do?

Think about the qualities that made Walter Payton a legend. It wasn't just his skill on the field but also his kindness, resilience, and dedication to helping others. What are some ways you can make a difference in your community? Maybe it's helping a friend in need, volunteering for a local charity, or even just being kind to others. Take a moment to reflect on how you can embody the spirit of Walter Payton in your own life. Write down three actions you can take to help others and make your community a better place. Who knows? You might just inspire someone else to do the same.

3.2 The Story of Jerry Rice: Dedication Leads to Success

Jerry Rice is a name that stands out in the world of football, not just because of his incredible talent but also because of his legendary work ethic. Imagine waking up before the sun rises, lacing up your running shoes, and hitting the hills for a grueling workout. That was Jerry Rice's offseason routine. Known for his rigorous training, Rice would run up steep hills to build his endurance and strength. These daily workouts weren't for the fainthearted. Rice believed that to be the best, you had to outwork everyone else. His dedication to training didn't just make him strong; it made him unstoppable on the field.

When you think of career milestones, Jerry Rice's list is like a highlight reel of football greatness. He played in three Super Bowls with the San Francisco 49ers, winning all three and earning the Super Bowl MVP award in one of them. Imagine catching 11 passes for 215 yards and a touchdown in a single Super Bowl game—that's exactly what Rice did in Super Bowl XXIII (23). Throughout his career, Rice set multiple records, including the most career touchdowns (208) and the most career receiving yards (22,895). These numbers are mind-blowing and reflect not just his talent but also his consistency and ability to perform at the highest level year after year.

What set Jerry Rice apart from his peers was his philosophy about hard work and preparation. He believed that success wasn't just about talent but about putting in the effort and being prepared for every game. Rice would meticulously study game footage, analyzing his opponents to find their weaknesses. This level of preparation allowed him to anticipate their moves, keeping him a step ahead on the field. Rice's work ethic extended beyond the physical; it was a mental game too. He always pushed himself to be better. This relentless drive is what made him one of the greatest wide receivers in NFL history.

Jerry Rice's playing days are over, but his impact continues. He has become a mentor and inspiration for younger players, showing them that hard work and dedication can lead to greatness. Many NFL players look up to Rice and try to copy his work ethic and commitment to the game. Rice's legacy is not just in the records he set but in the example he set for others. He has also been involved in various charitable activities, using his platform to give back to the community. Rice's influence continues to be felt, inspiring the next generation of football players to strive for excellence both on and off the field.

> **Interactive Exercise: Create Your Own Training Plan**
> Think about Jerry Rice's dedication to his offseason workouts. Now, imagine you're creating your own training plan to become better at football or any sport you love. Write down three exercises you would include in your daily routine and explain why you chose them. Maybe it's running hills like Rice for endurance, practicing your catching skills, or working on your agility with ladder drills. This exercise will help you think about the importance of consistent hard work and how you can apply it to your own goals.

3.3 Sarah Fuller: Breaking Barriers in Football

Imagine being the first woman to play in a Power 5 college football game. That's exactly what Sarah Fuller did, making history and showing that barriers are meant to be broken. On November 28, 2020, she stepped onto the field as the kicker for the Vanderbilt Commodores, marking a significant moment for gender equality in sports. Picture the crowd watching in awe as she took her place, not just as a player but as a symbol of progress. Fuller's achievement wasn't just about scoring points; it was about challenging and opening doors for future generations of female athletes.

Before her groundbreaking moment in football, Sarah Fuller was already making waves in another sport. At Vanderbilt University, she was a standout soccer player known for her skills as a goalkeeper. Her journey to football began somewhat unexpectedly. Due to COVID-19,

Vanderbilt's football team faced a shortage of players, and they needed a kicker. Fresh off a Southeastern Conference (SEC) championship with the soccer team, Fuller was asked to step in. She accepted the challenge, showing incredible adaptability and courage. Transitioning from soccer to football wasn't easy, but Fuller's athleticism and determination helped her succeed. Her story is a testament to the idea that stepping out of your comfort zone can lead to extraordinary opportunities.

The media and public reaction to Sarah Fuller's participation in football was immense. Her debut was covered by news outlets around the world, sparking conversations about women in traditionally male-dominated sports. Some people were thrilled and inspired by her achievement, seeing it as a step forward for gender equality. Others, however, were skeptical or critical, questioning whether she belonged on the field. Regardless of the mixed reactions, Fuller's presence in the game ignited important discussions about inclusion and opportunity in sports. She became a role model for young girls everywhere by showing them that they, too, could pursue their dreams, no matter the obstacles.

Sarah Fuller's influence didn't stop with her historic game. She has continued to advocate for women in sports, using her platform to speak out about gender equality and the importance of representation. Fuller actively participates in events and campaigns that promote women's sports, encouraging young athletes to break down barriers and strive for their goals. Her role as a spokesperson for gender equality has solidified her place as a trailblazer, inspiring others to follow in her footsteps. Fuller's journey is far from over, and her ongoing efforts continue to make a positive impact on the world of sports.

3.4 More Women in Football: Expanding the Game

More pioneering women have joined football teams in various roles in recent years. **Jen Welter**, for instance, became the first female coach in the NFL when she joined the Arizona Cardinals' coaching staff. She didn't just break barriers; she smashed through them, proving that women have a place in coaching at the highest levels of the sport. **Katie Sowers** followed suit as an offensive assistant coach for the San Francisco 49ers, making headlines and inspiring many young girls to dream big. These women had to overcome a ton of obstacles to get where they are today.

Being a woman in football isn't always easy. Women like Welter and Sowers faced numerous challenges, including prejudice and resistance from those who believed football should remain a men-only sport. They often had to prove themselves over and over again, fighting for respect and recognition in a world that wasn't always welcoming. Imagine constantly being doubted or questioned just because of your gender. Despite these hurdles, they persisted, showing incredible resilience and determination. They had to be tougher, smarter, and more prepared than anyone else, all while dealing with the added pressure of being trailblazers in a male-dominated field.

Their achievements haven't gone unnoticed. Jen Welter's groundbreaking role with the Arizona Cardinals opened doors and changed perceptions about women in coaching. Katie Sowers made history by becoming the first woman coach in the Super Bowl, where she helped guide the 49ers to a fantastic season. These milestones have earned them recognition and respect within the football community and beyond. Their success stories are paving the way for future generations of women who aspire to be part of professional football, whether as players, coaches, or in other roles. They've shown that with hard work and determination, anything is possible.

These stories are incredibly inspiring, especially for young girls who love football but might feel like it's not a sport for them. Seeing women succeed at the highest levels of football can ignite a spark, showing them that they, too, can achieve their dreams. It's about more than just playing the game; it's about breaking stereotypes and challenging societal norms. When girls see someone like Katie Sowers coaching in the Super Bowl, they realize that football isn't just for boys. It's for anyone with passion and dedication. These role models encourage young girls to pursue their interests confidently, knowing they belong on the field just as much as anyone else.

> **Reflection Section: Your Own Path**
> Think about the pioneers and players along with the challenges they've overcome. Now, reflect on your passions and interests. What barriers might you face, and how can you work to overcome them? Write down one goal you have and three steps you can take to achieve it. Remember, just like these men and women, you have the power to break down barriers and inspire others along the way. Use this exercise to think about how you can pursue your dreams and make a difference, no matter what challenges come your way.

3.5 Overcoming Challenges: Lessons from Doug Flutie

When you think about quarterbacks, you probably imagine tall players with strong arms who can see over the defensive line easily. But Doug Flutie, standing at just 5'10", faced the constant challenge of proving that height wasn't everything in football. Throughout his early career, Flutie had to deal with doubters who thought he was too short to play quarterback at a high level. Coaches and scouts often overlooked his talent, focusing instead on his stature. Yet Flutie never let these obstacles stop him. He worked tirelessly to better his skills, showing his agility, quick thinking, and tremendous heart on the field.

One of the most unforgettable moments in Flutie's career is the famous "Hail Flutie" pass. Picture this: It's 1984, and Boston College is playing against the University of Miami. With just seconds left on the clock and his team trailing, Flutie scrambled to avoid defenders and launched a desperate 64-yard pass into the end zone. The ball sailed through the air, and as it descended, wide receiver Gerard Phelan caught it, securing an incredible last second victory. This play didn't just win the game; it cemented Flutie's reputation as a clutch performer who could deliver under pressure. The "Hail Flutie" pass is still remembered as one of the greatest moments in college football history.

Flutie's adaptability was another key to his success. Throughout his career, he played for various teams in different leagues, including the NFL, CFL (Canadian Football League), and even a stint in the USFL (United States Football League). Each league presented its own set of challenges, but Flutie's ability to adjust his playing style and learn new systems showcased his resilience and flexibility. In the CFL, he became a legend, winning multiple championships and earning numerous MVP awards. When he returned to the NFL, he continued to prove his doubters wrong by leading teams to victories and earning a Pro Bowl selection. Flutie's ability to thrive in different environments and overcome adversity made him a truly unique player.

Beyond his on field achievements, Doug Flutie's legacy includes his significant charitable work. Inspired by his son who has autism, Flutie started the Doug Flutie Jr. Foundation for Autism. This organization provides support to families affected by autism, funding educational programs, advocacy initiatives, and research. Flutie's commitment to his foundation reflects his character off the field—dedicated, compassionate, and driven to make a difference. Through his foundation, he has touched countless lives, helping families navigate the challenges of autism and providing them with much-needed resources and support.

Flutie's story is a powerful example of how determination, adaptability, and a big heart can overcome even the tallest obstacles. His career reminds us that no matter the challenges we face, with hard work and perseverance, we can achieve greatness and make a positive impact on the world.

3.6 Lesser-Known Heroes: Players Who Made a Difference

When you think about football heroes, names like Patrick Mahomes and Dak Prescott might come to mind. But there are many players whose contributions are just as impactful, even if they don't always make the headlines. Take **Steve Tasker**, for example. He wasn't the biggest star, but his role on special teams for the Buffalo Bills was critical. Known for his incredible speed and tackling ability, Tasker became one of the best special teams players in NFL history. He earned seven Pro Bowl selections, a rare feat for someone in his position. Tasker's journey wasn't filled with glitzy stats or flashy plays, but his dedication and skill made him a key player for his team.

Defining moments often come in the form of unforgettable plays or standout seasons. For Steve Tasker, one such moment was during a playoff game against the Cleveland Browns, where he blocked a punt that changed the momentum of the game. His ability to make game-changing plays in crucial moments earned him respect and admiration from fans and peers alike. **Kurt Warner**'s defining moment was undoubtedly the 1999 season, when he led the Rams to a Super Bowl win with his incredible passing and leadership. Nicknamed "The Greatest Show on Turf," that season showcased Warner's talent and solidified his place in football history.

Off the field, both Tasker and Warner have made significant contributions to their communities. Steve Tasker has been involved in various charitable activities, including youth football camps and educational programs. His commitment to giving back has made him a role model for young athletes. Kurt Warner and his wife, Brenda, founded the First Things First Foundation, which focuses on supporting those in need. The foundation helps with everything from building homes for low-income families to organizing trips for children with life-threatening illnesses. Warner's efforts off the field highlight the importance of using one's platform to make a positive impact.

Another person who overcame adversity to get to where he is now is **Porter Ellett**. After a childhood accident, he was left with one arm. This did not stop him from playing baseball and basketball throughout high school. He also faced bullying growing up. There are times that people say unkind things around him even now. Ellett uses those things to keep getting better. His hard work, dedication, and belief in himself has driven his career, and he is now a quality control coach for the Kansas City Chiefs.

Their journeys were not without challenges. These stories of perseverance show that success is not always about being the biggest or fastest; sometimes, it's about having the heart and determination to keep going, no matter the odds.

Their stories remind us that greatness can come from anywhere. Whether you dream of making it big in football or pursuing another passion, remember these names. Their achievements on the field and contributions off it prove that with hard work, perseverance, and a bit of faith, you can make a difference and achieve your dreams.

3.7 Young Talents in NFL History: Prodigies of the Sport

Imagine being just 19 years old and already playing in the NFL. That's what happened to **Amobi Okoye**, who entered the league at an age when most of us are still figuring out high school. Born in Nigeria, Okoye moved to the United States and quickly fell in love with football. His rapid rise through the ranks was nothing short of extraordinary. He finished high school at 16 and then went on to play college football at the University of Louisville. By the time he was drafted by the Houston Texans, he was the youngest player ever to be selected in the first round of the NFL Draft. His story is a testament to what can be achieved with talent and hard work, no matter how young you are.

Starting a career in the NFL at such a young age brings a lot of pressure. Imagine balancing the demands of professional football with the typical challenges faced by teenagers. Young talents like Amobi Okoye often have to grow up fast, dealing with the expectations of coaches, teammates, and fans. They have to manage the spotlight and the constant scrutiny that comes with being a prodigy. Some handle it well, thriving under the pressure, while others struggle to find their footing. But what sets successful young players apart is their ability to stay focused and resilient, even when the stakes are high. They lean on their support systems—coaches, family, and friends—to help them navigate the ups and downs of their early careers.

If you fast-forward a bit, you might wonder where these young talents are now. Amobi Okoye, for instance, faced some challenges during his NFL career, including injuries that eventually led him to step away from the game. But life doesn't end when a football career does. Okoye has since focused on giving back to the community, engaging in charitable efforts and utilizing his platform to inspire others. He founded the Amobi Okoye Foundation, which aims to provide educational and athletic opportunities for young people. His story shows that even after the NFL, there's a lot of life to live and many ways to make a positive impact.

Another young talent worth mentioning is **Trevor Lawrence**, who entered the NFL with a ton of hype. Known for his incredible performance at Clemson University, where he led his team to a national championship, Lawrence was the first overall pick in the 2021 NFL Draft. His transition to the NFL was watched closely by fans and analysts alike. The pressure on him was immense, but Lawrence managed to stay grounded, focusing on improving his game and handling the expectations with maturity beyond his years. His ability to manage the spotlight and continue to grow as a player has made him a role model for aspiring athletes everywhere.

These stories remind us that talent alone isn't enough. Young players must also have the mental toughness to handle the pressures that come with early success. They need to be adaptable by learning from their experiences and staying resilient in the face of challenges. Whether they go on to have long NFL careers or find new paths, their journeys are filled with valuable lessons. It's inspiring to see how these young talents have not only made a name for themselves on the field but have also used their experiences to help others and make a difference in the world.

3.8 More Football Legends: Humble Start to Greatness

Imagine a kid just like you playing football in the backyard, dreaming of one day making it to the NFL. That's how many football legends started. Take **Brett Favre**, for example. Growing up in a small town in Mississippi, Favre didn't have the fancy equipment or big stadiums. He played in fields and practiced with his family. His dad was his high school coach, and Favre often had to play multiple positions because the team was so small. Despite these humble beginnings, Favre's passion and hard work eventually led him to become one of the greatest quarterbacks in NFL history.

When you think about how these players first got involved in football, it often starts with a simple love for the game. **Drew Brees**, another legendary quarterback, began playing flag football as a kid. He wasn't always the biggest or the fastest, but he had a strong arm and a fierce competitive spirit. Early on, Brees faced challenges like being overlooked due to his size. But he kept practicing, improving his skills little by little. His first big success came in high school when he led his team to a state championship. That victory was a turning point, showing him that with dedication, he could achieve great things.

Mentors and role models play a crucial role in the development of young athletes. For many football legends, having someone to guide and encourage them made all the difference. Take **Emmitt Smith**, for instance. Growing up in Florida, Smith looked up to his high school coach, who saw potential in him and pushed him to be his best. Smith's coach taught him the importance of discipline and hard work, lessons that stayed with him throughout his career. These early influences helped shape Smith into the NFL's all-time leading rusher, proving that the support and guidance of a mentor can be incredibly powerful.

So, what's the message here? It's simple; no matter where you start, with passion and dedication you can achieve greatness. Many of the football legends we admire today began their journeys in small towns, playing on makeshift fields. They faced challenges, doubters, and setbacks, but they never gave up. They kept pushing forward, fueled by their love for the game and a belief in their abilities. The same can be true for you. Whether it's football, another sport, or any other passion, the key is to keep working hard, staying focused, and believing in yourself.

These stories remind us that greatness often starts in the most ordinary places and show us that with the right mindset, anyone can overcome obstacles and reach their goals. So, the next time you're out playing football or working on a project, remember that the legends you look up to were once just like you. They took their first steps with determination and hope, and you can too.

In this chapter, we've explored the beginnings of football legends, their early challenges, and the mentors who guided them. These stories are a powerful reminder that greatness is within reach for anyone willing to work for it. As we move to the next chapter, get ready to discover how football can teach valuable life skills and boost your confidence.

Chapter 4

FOOTBALL, FITNESS, AND HEALTH

Ever wonder how pro football players get geared up for games? It's all about their training routines, both on and off the field. Let's dive into what makes them the incredible athletes they are, and how you can learn to boost your own game based on their dedication and hard work.

4.1 Training Routines of Top Football Players

When it comes to training, professional football players have schedules that might make your head spin. Their days are packed with activities designed to make them stronger, faster, and smarter on the field. A typical day often starts early, around 6 AM. Imagine waking up, grabbing a quick, nutritious breakfast, and heading straight to the gym. Morning workouts usually focus on strength training. Players lift weights to build muscle and improve their power. They might do bench presses, squats, and deadlifts, all exercises that target different muscle groups. After lifting, there's usually a quick break for a protein-packed snack to refuel their bodies.

Midmorning is often dedicated to team meetings and film study. This is where players watch footage of their previous games and upcoming opponents. They analyze plays, learn from their mistakes, and develop strategies for their next game. It's like doing homework but for football. After lunch, it's back to the field for practice. This can include everything from running drills to practicing specific plays. Players work on their speed, agility, and technique, making sure they're in sync with their teammates. The day usually wraps up with a cooldown and some stretching to keep their muscles flexible and prevent injuries.

During the off-season, training routines look a bit different. Without the pressure of upcoming games, players focus more on building their overall fitness and working on specific skills. This is the time for intense weight training to build muscle strength and endurance. Players might also take up other sports like basketball or swimming to keep their workouts fun and varied. These activities help improve their cardiovascular health and keep them in top shape. The off-season is also a great time for players to work on any weaknesses they noticed during the season. They may want to improve their throwing accuracy or get faster on their feet. The focus is on becoming a better all-around athlete.

Strength and conditioning are at the core of any football training program. Players engage in exercises that target both their upper and lower body. For example, squats and lunges are essential for building leg strength, which is important for running and jumping. Upper body exercises like bench presses and shoulder presses help build the muscle needed for blocking and tackling. Core exercises like planks and Russian twists are vital for stability and balance. These workouts aren't just about lifting as much weight as possible. Proper form is crucial to avoid injuries and ensure that each exercise targets the right muscles.

Recovery practices are just as important as the workouts themselves. After a hard day of training, players need to give their bodies time to heal and rebuild. This starts with getting plenty of sleep. Most athletes aim for at least 8 hours of sleep each night, as this is when the body does most of its repair work. Rest days are also built into their schedules, giving muscles a chance to recover from the strain of training. Techniques like massage and foam rolling can help relieve muscle tension and improve circulation. Cold baths or ice baths are another popular recovery method. Sitting in cold water helps reduce inflammation and speed up recovery, so players are ready to go for their next training session.

Training like a pro football player is no small feat. It requires dedication, hard work, and a commitment to constant improvement. But by understanding their routines, you can start incorporating some of these practices into your own training. Whether playing football, another sport, or just trying to stay active, these tips can help you reach your goals and become the best version of yourself.

4.2 Eating Right: Nutrition Tips for Young Athletes

Alright, let's talk about something super important for anyone who loves playing football or any sport—eating right. Imagine your body is like a high performance car. To run smoothly and efficiently, it needs the right kind of fuel. That's where nutrition comes in. Basic nutrition boils down to three key nutrients: **carbohydrates**, **proteins**, and **fats**. Carbohydrates are like the fuel that gives you quick energy. Foods like pasta, bread, and fruits are packed with carbs and are great for giving you the energy to run, jump, and tackle. Proteins are the building blocks for your muscles. They help repair and grow your muscles after a tough practice or game. Think chicken, fish, beans, and nuts. Finally, fats aren't the bad guys they're often made out to be. Healthy fats, found in foods like avocados, nuts, and olive oil, provide long-lasting energy and help keep your body running smoothly.

Staying hydrated is just as important as eating the right foods. Imagine playing a game on a hot day without drinking enough water—you'd feel tired, sluggish, and maybe even dizzy. That's because water is vital for keeping your body cool and helping your muscles work properly. Before a game or practice, make sure you drink plenty of water. During the activity, take small sips regularly, especially if you're sweating a lot. And after you're done, drink more water to help your body recover, but spread it out so you don't drink too much, too fast. Sports drinks can also be helpful, especially if you're exercising for a long time, as they replace electrolytes lost through sweat. But water should always be your go-to drink.

Planning your meals around your training is a game-changer. Before you hit the field, you need a meal that fuels you up without weighing you down. Think of a balanced meal that includes carbs, proteins, and a little bit of fat. For example, a turkey sandwich on whole-grain bread with a side of fruit is perfect. If you're in a rush, a banana and a handful of nuts can do the trick. After practice or a game, it's all about recovery. Your muscles need protein to repair and carbs to replenish the energy you've burned. A simple meal like grilled chicken with brown rice and veggies is fantastic. If you need a quick after workout snack, try a smoothie with yogurt and fruit.

Snacking smart is key to keeping your energy levels up throughout the day. Instead of reaching for chips or candy, try to choose snacks that are both tasty and healthy, and that ideally combine carbs with protein and healthy fats.

> **Healthy Snack Ideas:**
> - Apple slices with peanut butter
> - Greek yogurt with honey and granola
> - Trail mix with nuts, seeds, and dried fruit
> - Cheese stick and a piece of fruit
> - Smoothie with yogurt and fruit

Eating right isn't just about what you eat but also about when you eat. Timing your meals and snacks to align with your training and game schedule can make a big difference in how you feel and perform. Remember, food is your fuel, and the better you fuel your body, the better you'll feel on and off the field. So the next time you're getting ready for a big game or even just a practice, think about what you're putting into your body. Making smart food choices can help you play your best and keep you feeling great.

4.3 Staying Active: Exercises for Off-Season Training

Staying in shape during the off-season is super important for any athlete, even if you're not playing games or having regular practices. This is the time to keep your body ready for action without burning yourself out. Think of it as maintaining your engine so it's ready to roar when the season starts again. You can mix things up with a variety of activities to keep it fun and interesting. **Running**, **biking**, or **swimming** can be great ways to stay active. These activities keep your heart pumping and your muscles working while giving you a break from the usual football drills. It's like taking a scenic route instead of the same old road—you're still moving ahead toward a goal, but in a different and refreshing way.

Cross-training is a fantastic way to stay fit and avoid getting bored. It just means mixing different types of exercises to work various parts of your body and improve your overall fitness. For example, swimming is excellent for building endurance and strengthening your entire body without putting too much strain on your joints. Cycling is another great option, as it boosts your cardiovascular health and builds leg strength. These activities not only make you a better athlete but also help prevent overuse injuries that can happen when you focus too much on one sport. Imagine how cool it would be to have stronger legs from cycling that also make you even faster on the football field!

Flexibility and mobility workouts are crucial for keeping your body in top shape and preventing injuries. You don't want to be that player who pulls a muscle just because you didn't stretch enough. **Yoga** is a fantastic way to enhance your flexibility. It involves a series of poses that stretch and strengthen different muscle groups, helping you become more flexible and balanced overall. Dynamic **stretching** routines, which involve moving stretches like leg swings and arm circles, are also great for improving mobility. These exercises prepare your muscles for the movements you'll make during games and practices, reducing the risk of injuries. Think of it as oiling your joints so everything moves smoothly.

Staying active doesn't always mean sticking to a strict workout routine. Sometimes, the best way to keep fit is by **having fun**. Playing other sports with friends or family can be a great way to stay active without feeling like a chore. Basketball, soccer, or even a game of tag can keep your body moving and your mind engaged. These activities not only provide a good workout but also help develop different skills that can benefit your football game. For instance, playing basketball can improve your hand-eye coordination and agility, making you a more versatile athlete. Plus, having fun with friends and family keeps your motivation high and makes staying active something you look forward to.

> **Fun Fitness Activities:**
> - Playing basketball or soccer with friends
> - Going for a swim at the local pool
> - Riding your bike around the neighborhood
> - Joining a recreational sports league
> - Having a dance-off with your family

Maintaining fitness during the off-season is all about keeping your body in shape while enjoying a variety of activities. Cross-training with different sports, focusing on flexibility and mobility, and having fun with friends and family are all great ways to stay active. So, whether you're swimming, cycling, or just playing a game of tag, remember that staying active is key to staying healthy.

4.4 The Importance of Mental Health in Sports

When you think about playing football, you probably imagine the physical challenges—running, tackling, and scoring touchdowns. But just as important is the mental side of the game. **Mental toughness** is what helps athletes stay focused and bounce back from setbacks. Imagine you're in a game and your team is down by a few points. Instead of giving up, you dig deep, stay positive, and keep pushing forward. That's mental toughness. Developing this kind of resilience takes practice. Start by setting small, achievable goals. Each time you reach one, you build confidence and mental strength. Also, keep a **positive mindset.** When things get tough, remind yourself of past successes and how hard you've worked. This kind of self-talk can keep you motivated even when the going gets tough.

Stress can creep up on you, especially when you're balancing school, sports, and other activities. Managing stress is crucial for staying healthy and performing well. One effective way to manage stress is through **mindfulness meditation.** To practice this, you just need a few minutes to yourself, although you can do it as long as you need, when you have the time. Find a quiet spot, sit down, close your eyes, and just breathe. Turn your attention to your body. Feel the air going in and out of your nose and diaphragm. Feel the weight of your closed eyelids. Relax your face muscles, shoulders, and legs. Take deep breaths in and out, focusing only on the movement happening in your body. Right before ending your meditation, you might give yourself a one or two sentence quiet pep talk. Something simple like "I can do this." Even just a few minutes of this can help you feel calmer and more focused. Another great technique is **deep breathing exercises.** This is easy to do even if you're around other people. To practice, take a deep breath in through your nose, hold it for a few seconds, and then slowly exhale through your mouth. This can help slow your heart rate and calm your mind. **Visualizing success** is another tool top athletes use to help them stay prepared and confident. Close your eyes and picture yourself making that perfect pass or doing well on the test. Something that can be hard to do is to **stay present and focused on the moment.** Instead of worrying about what might go wrong, concentrate on what you need to do right now. Break the game down into small, manageable pieces and focus on each play as it comes. You can also apply this while studying or working on a hard assignment. And don't forget about the importance of **sleep.** Getting enough rest is crucial for your body and mind to recover. Aim for at least 8 hours of sleep each night to feel refreshed and ready for the day. Our mental health is just as important as our physical health. Finding ways to get through stressful times is something we can all use throughout our whole life.

Having a **strong support system** can make a huge difference in your mental health. Coaches, family, and teammates can provide the emotional support and advice you need to navigate the ups and downs of life. Imagine having a tough practice and feeling down. Talking to your coach can help you understand what went wrong and how to improve. Your family can offer encouragement and remind you of your strengths. Teammates can share their own experiences and help you feel less alone. Knowing that you have people who believe in you can boost your confidence and help you stay motivated. Don't be afraid to reach out to your support system when you need it. Whether it's a pep talk from your coach, a hug from a family member, or a high-five from a teammate, these moments of support can keep you going.

4.5 Handling Injuries: Prevention and Care

In football, injuries can happen even to the best players. Knowing how to handle them can make a big difference in how quickly you recover and get back on the field. Let's talk about some common football injuries and what you can do to prevent and care for them. One of the most common injuries is a sprain, which happens when you stretch or tear the ligaments around a joint like your ankle or wrist. Imagine running down the field and suddenly twisting your ankle. That sharp pain you feel is likely a sprain. Another frequent injury is a concussion, which occurs when you get a hard hit to the head, causing your brain to shake inside your skull. Symptoms might include headaches, dizziness, and confusion. Then there's the classic bruise, which happens when you get hit hard enough to break small blood vessels under your skin, causing a black-and-blue mark. While bruises are usually minor, they can still be pretty painful.

Preventing injuries starts with a proper warm-up. Before you hit the field, spend a few minutes doing dynamic stretches like leg swings and arm circles to get your blood flowing and muscles ready for action. These exercises help increase your flexibility and reduce the risk of pulls and strains. Using the correct technique is also crucial. Whether you're tackling, blocking, or running, make sure you're doing it the right way to avoid unnecessary strain on your body. For instance, when tackling, always keep your head up to prevent head and neck injuries. Wearing appropriate protective gear, like helmets, shoulder pads, and mouthguards, is another key factor. These items are designed to absorb impact and protect your body from serious harm.

Knowing some basic first aid can be a lifesaver when injuries happen. One of the most effective methods for treating sprains and minor injuries is the RICE method: Rest, Ice, Compression, and Elevation. If you sprain your ankle, stop playing immediately and rest. Apply ice to the injured area for 20 minutes to reduce swelling. Use a compression bandage to support the joint and minimize swelling, then elevate your ankle above your heart level to help reduce the inflammation. For cuts and scrapes, clean the wound with water and apply an antiseptic to prevent infection. Cover it with a clean bandage and keep an eye on it to make sure it heals properly.

Sometimes, injuries are more serious and require professional medical attention. But how do you know when it's time to see a doctor? If you experience severe pain or swelling or can't put weight on the injured area, it's a good idea to get it checked out. For head injuries, like concussions, seek medical help if you have symptoms like headaches, dizziness, vomiting, or confusion. If you're unsure, talk to your family or coach. It's important not to play through serious injuries, as this can make things worse and prolong your recovery time. Always listen to your body and take injuries seriously.

Understanding common football injuries and how to prevent and care for them is crucial for staying safe on the field. By warming up properly, using the proper techniques, wearing protective gear, and knowing basic first aid, you can reduce your risk of injury and enjoy the game to the fullest. And remember, if something feels wrong, don't hesitate to seek professional help. **Your health and safety should always come first.**

4.6 Balancing School and Sports: Tips for Student-Athletes

Balancing school and sports can feel like juggling a bunch of footballs in the air. One of the biggest tricks to managing everything is mastering time management. Picture your day as a big puzzle. You need to make all the pieces fit perfectly. Start by creating a schedule that includes both your schoolwork and sports commitments. Write down your classes, practice times, and game days. Then, look for pockets of free time where you can do homework or study sessions. Maybe you have a free period at school or some time before practice. Use these moments wisely to keep up with your studies. Breaking your day into manageable chunks helps ensure you're not overwhelmed and can stay on top of both your academic and athletic responsibilities.

Once you have your schedule sorted out, it's important to set your priorities straight. Think of your tasks as a football playbook. Just like in a game, some plays are more critical than others. **Remember, being a student-athlete means you're a student first.** Make a list of what needs to get done each day and rank them by importance. Homework and studying for tests should be at the top of your list. Next, consider your sports commitments. Practice and games are essential, but they should never overshadow your schoolwork. By setting clear priorities, you can focus on what's most important and avoid last-minute cramming or missed assignments.

For those days when your schedule is jam-packed, having effective study tips up your sleeve can make a big difference. One great technique is to use travel time wisely. If you're on the bus heading to an away game, bring your textbooks or notes and get some studying done. Another tip is to break your studying into smaller, focused sessions. Instead of trying to study for hours on end, set a timer for 20-30 minutes and focus on one subject. Take a short break, then move on to the next task. This method helps keep your mind fresh and prevents burnout. Also, find a quiet and comfortable place to study where you can concentrate without distractions.

Open communication with your teachers and coaches is key to balancing school and sports successfully. Imagine trying to play a game without knowing the plays or the rules—it would be chaos. The same goes for your academic and athletic life. Let your teachers know about your sports commitments, especially if you have games or practices that might conflict with schoolwork. Most teachers are understanding and can help you find ways to stay on track. The same goes for your coaches. If you have a big test coming up, talk to your coach about possibly adjusting your practice schedule or finding a compromise. Being upfront and honest about your commitments helps build trust and ensures everyone is on the same page.

Balancing school and sports is all about finding the right rhythm. With good time management, setting priorities, smart study techniques, and open communication, you can excel both in the classroom and on the field. Remember, being a student-athlete is a rewarding experience that teaches you valuable skills for life. So, embrace the challenge and enjoy the ride. You've got this!

Make a Difference with Your Review

Unlock the Power of Generosity
People who give without expecting anything in return, live happier lives. So, let's make a difference together!

Would you help someone just like you—curious about football but unsure where to start?

My mission is to make learning about football easy and fun for everyone.

But to reach more people, I need your help.

Most people choose books based on reviews. So, I'm asking you to help other kids learn more about football by leaving a review. It's not a test, costs nothing, and takes less than a minute but could change someone's football journey.

How to Share Your Thoughts
Writing a review can be quick and easy. You could share any of the following:
- Your favorite part of the book
- Something new you learned
- How it helped you understand football better
- Why you'd recommend it to other kids like you

To make a difference, simply scan the QR code or visit the link below and leave a review (make sure you ask for permission first :)

https://www.amazon.com/review/review-your-purchases/?asin=B0DV5DQ6BC

If you love helping others, you're my kind of person. Thank you from the bottom of my heart!

Lori – Blitz Books

Chapter 5
VALUES LEARNED THROUGH FOOTBALL

Values are like the rules in a game – they help guide us in how we play, both on and off the field. Learning values shape who you are, helping you to make good choices, work well with others, and feel proud of yourself.

5.1 Teamwork

Imagine you're in the middle of a thrilling football game. The score is tied, and there's only one minute left on the clock. You and your teammates huddle together, each person knowing exactly what they need to do to win. This moment is all about **teamwork**, one of the most important lessons football can teach us. Teamwork isn't just about playing a game; it's about learning how to work together to achieve a common goal, whether on the field or in everyday life. Each player has a specific role, and success depends on everyone doing their part. The quarterback needs to trust that the offensive line will protect them, while the wide receivers rely on the QB to deliver accurate passes. This level of teamwork translates to other areas of life, like working on school projects. Imagine you're assigned a group project. Just like in football, each member has a role. Someone might research, another might write, and someone else might create a presentation. By working together and trusting each other, you can create something amazing.

There are countless examples of teamwork making a critical difference in football games. One famous instance is the "Philly Special" play during Super Bowl LII (52). The Philadelphia Eagles were facing the New England Patriots, and the game was incredibly close. On a crucial fourth down, the Eagles executed a trick play where the quarterback, Nick Foles, actually caught a touchdown pass. This play required perfect timing and trust among the players, and it helped the Eagles secure their first Super Bowl victory. Such moments highlight how football is a game of collaboration, where every player's effort matters.

5.2 Trust

Building **trust** with teammates is essential for any football team. Trust develops through practice, communication, and shared experiences. When players practice together, they learn each other's strengths and weaknesses, building a bond that translates into better performance during games. Trust also plays a significant role in the success of a team. A quarterback needs to trust that their receivers will be in the right place at the right time, and the receivers need to trust that the quarterback will throw a catchable pass. This mutual trust strengthens the team's overall performance, making them more cohesive and effective.

5.3 Communication

Communication is another skill that's just as important on the football field as in everyday life. On the field, players constantly communicate—calling out plays, signaling routes, and making adjustments. This ability to communicate clearly and effectively is invaluable in school too, where you might need to work with classmates on projects or participate in group discussions. **Conflict resolution** and **cooperative problem-solving** can help with good communication. Disagreements can arise during games or practices, but learning to resolve these conflicts calmly and constructively helps maintain team harmony. Cooperative problem-solving can be vital when a team faces unexpected challenges, like a strong opposing defense. Players need to work together to find solutions, adjust their strategies, and support each other. This collaborative approach to problem-solving can be applied to any situation, from tackling a tough math problem to planning a school event. By working together and combining different perspectives, you can find creative solutions to challenges.

Teamwork is working together with others to achieve a common goal. **Trust** is the belief in the reliability, truth, ability, and strength in someone or something. **Communication** is the ability to interact with others to understand their points and to let them know what you want them to know. **Conflict resolution** is working with another to understand a problem or conflict and working together to solve it. **Cooperative problem-solving** is using conflict resolution in a team or group environment.

Interactive Exercise: Teamwork Reflection

Take a moment to think about a time when you worked as part of a team, either in sports, at school, or in another activity. Write down your answers to the following questions:

1. What was the goal of your team?

2. What role did you play in achieving that goal?

3. How did you and your teammates communicate and problem solve?

4. What challenges did you face, and how did you overcome them?

5. What did you learn from this experience that you can apply to future teamwork situations?

Reflecting on these questions can help you understand the importance of teamwork and how the skills you develop in football can benefit you in many other areas of life. Keep practicing these skills, and you'll become a stronger, more effective team player both on and off the field.

5.4 Leadership Skills Every Young Athlete Can Develop

Imagine being the player everyone looks up to, the one who keeps the team motivated and focused. That's what it means to be a leader in sports. Leadership on a football team is more than just being the best player. It's about inspiring your teammates, staying positive even when things aren't going well, and setting an example through your actions. Great football captains, like Trevor Lawrence or Russell Wilson, show these qualities every game. They lead with their words and their actions, encouraging everyone to give their best effort, no matter what the score.

Even if you're not the team captain, you can still be a leader. Leadership isn't about titles; it's about actions. You can demonstrate leadership by always giving your best effort in practice and games. Show up on time, listen to your coaches, and stay focused. Encourage your teammates when they're feeling down and celebrate their successes. For instance, if a teammate makes a great play, be the first to high-five them and shout, "Great job!" Simple acts like these can boost team morale and make everyone feel valued. Leadership is also about taking responsibility. If you make a mistake, own up to it and learn from it. Don't blame others or make excuses. By being accountable, you set a strong example for your teammates.

Good leaders share several key characteristics. **Integrity** is one of them. This means being honest and doing the right thing, even when no one is watching. A player like Larry Fitzgerald exemplified integrity. Known for his sportsmanship and dedication, he always played fair and respected his opponents. Accountability is another crucial trait. Leaders **take responsibility** for their actions. They don't shy away from admitting mistakes and work hard to improve. Aaron Donald, a great defensive end, was known for his accountability and relentless drive to be better. **Inspiration** is also vital. Leaders inspire others through their actions and words. They motivate their teammates to push harder and never give up. Think of Peyton Manning, who was known for his pep talks and ability to rally his team during tough times.

Parents and coaches play a significant role in developing leadership qualities in young athletes. One effective way to encourage leadership is by giving kids opportunities to take on responsibilities. For example, a coach might assign different players to lead warm-up exercises or organize team activities. This helps them learn how to guide and motivate others. Positive reinforcement is also crucial, such as praising young athletes when they show leadership qualities like encouraging teammates or showing good sportsmanship. This reinforces the behavior and makes them more likely to continue acting as leaders. Another tip is to provide examples of role models by sharing stories of great leaders in sports and discussing what makes them effective. Watching videos of inspirational speeches or reading about athletes who overcame challenges can inspire young players to develop their own leadership skills.

Interactive Exercise: Leadership Reflection

Think about a time when you saw someone show great leadership, either in football or any activity. Write down your answers to these questions:

1. What did the leader do that stood out to you?

2. How did their actions affect the team or group?

3. What qualities did they display that you admire?

4. How can you incorporate these qualities into your own behavior?

Reflecting on these questions can help you understand what makes a good leader and how you can develop these qualities yourself. Leadership isn't about being perfect; it's about striving to be the best version of yourself and helping others do the same. Keep practicing these skills, and you'll become a strong, inspiring leader both on and off the field.

Integrity is being honest and doing the right thing even if no one will know. **Taking responsibility** for your actions means admitting your mistakes, on purpose or not, and working to do better. Being **inspiring** within a team means giving positive words to others, helping others see the good they are doing, and contributing in a positive way to the team.

5.5 Fair Play: Learning Sportsmanship Early

Imagine playing a tough game where every move counts. You're giving it your all, but so are your opponents. **Sportsmanship** is playing fair, respecting others, and enjoying the game, no matter the outcome. It's about shaking hands with your opponent whether you win or lose and understanding that the game is bigger than just you. Good sportsmanship is crucial because it teaches us to respect others and value the spirit of the game. It's not just about winning; it's about how you play the game and how you treat your teammates and opponents.

Let's look at some moments in football history where players showed exceptional sportsmanship. One memorable example was when Larry Fitzgerald of the Arizona Cardinals congratulated the opposing team even after a heartbreaking loss. After the Pittsburgh Steelers scored a game winning touchdown during the 2009 Super Bowl, instead of sulking, Fitzgerald went over to the Steelers' sideline to congratulate them. This act of kindness and respect showed that he valued the effort and skill of his opponents, even in defeat. Another instance is when J.J. Watt, a defensive end known for his fierce competitiveness, helped an injured opponent get off the field during a game. These acts remind us that football is not just about the physical game but also about showing respect and kindness, no matter the circumstances.

Wins and losses are part of the game, and how you handle them says a lot about you. When you win, it's important to celebrate with grace. This means acknowledging the hard work of your teammates and respecting your opponents. Bragging or boasting can make others feel bad and take away from the joy of the victory. A simple "good game" to the other team can go a long way. On the flip side, losing can be tough, but it's important to handle it with dignity. Instead of getting angry or blaming others, think about what you can learn from the loss. Maybe there's a skill you can improve or a strategy that didn't work out. Expressing your emotions in a healthy way, like talking to a coach or teammate, can help you process the loss and move forward positively.

Being a good sport has many long-term benefits. One of the biggest is building lasting friendships. When you show respect and kindness on the field, you're more likely to make friends who appreciate those qualities. These friendships can extend beyond the game, creating a network of support and friendship. Good sportsmanship also earns you respect from others. Coaches, teammates, and even opponents will notice your positive attitude and fair play, which can lead to more opportunities like being chosen as team captain or receiving sportsmanship awards. Additionally, the values you learn through sportsmanship—like respect, empathy, and integrity—are qualities that will serve you well in all areas of life, from school to your future career.

Reflection Section: Sportsmanship in Action

Think about a time when you saw or experienced good sportsmanship, either in football or another activity. Write down your answers to these questions:

1. What happened during this moment of good sportsmanship?

2. How did it make you feel, or how did it impact the game?

3. What lessons can you take from this experience and apply to your own behavior?

Reflecting on these questions can help you understand the importance of sportsmanship and how you can practice it in your own life. Being a good sport is not just about the game; it's about being a kind and respectful person in everything you do. So, next time you're on the field or participating in any competition, remember to play fair, respect others, and enjoy the game.

5.6 Overcoming Challenges: What Football Teaches Us About Resilience

Imagine being down by three touchdowns in the fourth quarter of a championship game. Most people would think the game is over, but not the 2017 New England Patriots. They were trailing the Atlanta Falcons 28-3 in Super Bowl LI (51). With persistence and mental toughness, they managed an incredible comeback, scoring 25 unanswered points and winning in overtime. This historic victory wasn't just about skill; it was about resilience, the ability to keep pushing forward even when the odds are stacked against you.

> In football, resilience is a crucial trait. It's the mental toughness required to bounce back from injuries, mistakes, or tough losses.

Developing a **resilient mindset** means believing in your ability to overcome challenges. It's about persistence and never letting setbacks define you. One way to build this mindset is by setting small, achievable goals. Each time you reach one, you gain confidence and build momentum. Another tip is to **embrace failure** as part of the learning process. Instead of seeing mistakes as reasons to quit, view them as opportunities to improve. Remember, every great player has faced setbacks. What sets them apart is their ability to keep going, learn from their experiences, and come back even stronger.

Imagine you're having a rough season. Maybe you've lost a few games or missed some important plays. It's easy to feel discouraged, but this is when resilience matters most. Take a deep breath and remind yourself that setbacks are temporary. Focus on what you can control—your effort, attitude, and willingness to improve. Talk to your coach or teammates for support and advice. They've likely faced similar challenges and can offer valuable insights. By staying positive and persistent, you'll find that you're capable of achieving much more than you initially thought.

Reflection Section: Building Resilience

Think about a time when you faced a challenge, whether in sports, school, or another area of your life. Write down your answers to these questions:

1. What was the challenge you faced?

2. How did you feel at that moment?

3. What strategies did you use to overcome it?

4. What did you learn from the experience?

Reflecting on these questions can help you understand the importance of resilience and how you can apply it to future challenges. Remember, resilience isn't about never failing; it's about **getting back up** every time you do. Keep practicing these skills, and you'll become more resilient both on and off the field.

5.7 Setting Goals and Achieving Them Through Sports

Imagine you're getting ready for a big game, and you know exactly what you want to achieve. Maybe you want to score a touchdown or improve your blocking skills. Setting goals is like having a roadmap that guides you to success. One of the best ways to set goals is by using the SMART method. SMART stands for Specific, Measurable, Achievable, Relevant, and Time-bound. Let's break this down with an example. Suppose you want to become a faster runner. A specific goal would be,

"I want to improve my 40-yard dash time." It's measurable because you can time yourself. Make sure it's achievable; don't aim to cut your time in half overnight. Relevance ensures the goal matters to your football performance, and setting a deadline makes it time-bound, like aiming to achieve this in three months. By breaking down your goals into these parts, you'll have a clear path to follow.

Think about the great players who have set and achieved incredible goals. Take Peyton Manning, for example. When he joined the Denver Broncos, he aimed to break the single-season touchdown record. Manning didn't just wish for it; he set a specific goal, practiced relentlessly, and monitored his progress. In 2013, he threw 55 touchdown passes, setting a new NFL record. Another inspiring story is that of Alex Smith. After suffering a life-threatening leg injury, many thought his career was over. But Smith set a goal to return to the NFL. Through determination, he worked tirelessly in rehab, tracking his small victories along the way. His return to the field was nothing short of miraculous, showcasing the power of goal setting and perseverance.

Monitoring your progress is crucial when working towards your goals. One effective method is keeping a training diary. Write down your daily workouts, what you ate, and how you felt. This helps you see patterns and make adjustments as needed. For instance, if you notice you perform better on days you eat a particular breakfast, you can make that part of your routine. Regular check-ins with your coach are also valuable. They can provide feedback on your progress and suggest adjustments to your training plan. Celebrate your small victories along the way, like shaving a fraction of a second off your sprint time or mastering a new technique. These milestones keep you motivated and show you're on the right track.

Sometimes, despite our best efforts, goals need to be adjusted. Maybe you set a goal to improve your passing accuracy, but an injury forces you to focus on recovery instead. It's important to be flexible and realistic. Adjusting your goals doesn't mean giving up; it means being smart about your approach. For example, if you're injured, you might shift your focus to mental aspects of the game, like studying playbooks or visualizing successful plays. This way you stay engaged and continue progressing, even if your original goal is temporarily on hold. Always reassess your goals based on new information or changing circumstances to ensure they remain relevant and achievable.

Goal setting is a powerful tool that helps athletes focus, stay motivated, and achieve their dreams. By setting SMART goals, learning from the achievements of others, and regularly monitoring and adjusting your progress, you can turn your ambitions into reality. Whether you're aiming to improve your skills on the football field or achieve something in another area of your life, these techniques will guide you every step of the way.

5.8 The Role of Discipline in Football Success

Imagine waking up early on a Saturday morning when you'd rather stay in bed. Instead, you get up, lace up your cleats, and head to practice. This is what disciplined training and preparation look like. Discipline in football means sticking to a routine, even when it's tough. It's about going to every practice, listening to your coach, and putting in the effort to improve your skills. This **dedication** is what separates good players from great ones. When you consistently show up and work hard, you build the foundation for success on the field. It's like stacking bricks to build a strong wall; each training session adds to your strength, skill, and confidence.

Self-discipline and **self-control** play a crucial role in maintaining focus and executing game plans under pressure. Imagine you're in a tight game, and the clock is ticking down. You feel the pressure, but you need to stay focused. Self-discipline helps you control your emotions and concentrate on the task at hand. It means not letting frustration or excitement cloud your judgment. Think of Patrick Mahomes, known for his calm demeanor even in the most intense moments. His ability to stay composed and make smart decisions is a result of years of practicing self-discipline. It's about doing what needs to be done, even when it's hard or you're tempted to take the easy way out.

The consequences of not being disciplined can be severe. Picture a game where a star player loses their cool and commits a costly penalty, leading to their team losing yardage or even the game. This lack of discipline can let down the entire team. Take the example of a player who skips practice because they think they're already good enough. When game day comes, they might find themselves out of sync with their teammates and missing crucial plays. This happened to a famous player once, who skipped practices and ended up fumbling the ball in a critical game, costing his team a chance at the playoffs. These scenarios highlight the importance of staying disciplined and committed to your training and your team.

Becoming more disciplined is a skill that can be developed with practice. Start by setting routines. For instance, create a daily schedule that includes time for homework, practice, and rest. Stick to this routine as much as possible. Setting rules for yourself, like limiting screen time or prioritizing your tasks, can help you stay focused. Another tip is to practice **self-regulation**. When you feel frustrated or tempted to slack off, take a deep breath and remind yourself of your goals. Visualization can be a powerful tool at times like this. Picture yourself succeeding because you stayed disciplined and followed through with your commitments. This mental exercise can strengthen your resolve and keep you on track.

Another practical tip for young athletes is to **break down your goals** into smaller, manageable tasks. Instead of focusing on becoming the best player, aim to improve one specific skill each week, like your passing accuracy or sprint speed. This makes the process less overwhelming and allows you to see progress more clearly. Celebrate these small victories to keep yourself motivated. Additionally, find a role model who exemplifies discipline, whether it's a professional athlete or someone you know personally. Study their habits and try to add some of their practices into your own routine.

Discipline in football and in life is about making consistent, focused efforts towards your goals. It's about showing up, putting in the work, and staying committed even when it's tough. By developing this trait, you not only improve your performance on the field but also build a strong foundation for success in all areas of your life. Whether you're aiming to excel in football, school, or any other endeavor, discipline is the key that will help you unlock your full potential and achieve your dreams.

5.9 Learning from Mistakes: Feedback on the Field

Playing football is a lot like riding a bike—you're going to fall many times before you get the hang of it. Mistakes are a natural part of learning and improving. They're like little signposts pointing out what you need to work on. Think about it; if you never dropped a pass, how would you know you need to practice your catching? **Normalizing mistakes** means understanding that everyone, even the best players, makes errors. Instead of feeling bad about them, use mistakes as opportunities to get better. Imagine each mistake as a step on a ladder, helping you climb higher and higher towards your goals.

Constructive feedback from coaches and teammates is one of the best tools for improvement. It's like having a mirror that shows you what you can't see yourself. When your coach tells you to keep your eye on the ball when catching, they're not criticizing you; they're helping you improve. Listen carefully to what they say and try to apply their advice. Feedback from peers is also valuable. Maybe a teammate notices you're positioning yourself too far back during a play. By listening and making adjustments, you can turn those observations into strengths. Remember, feedback is meant to help you, not to bring you down.

Self-analysis is another powerful way to learn from mistakes. Keeping a game diary can be incredibly helpful. After each practice or game, write down what went well and what didn't. Reflect on why certain plays worked and why others didn't. This helps you identify patterns and areas where you can improve. Video reviews are also a fantastic tool. Watching recordings of your games allows you to see things you might have missed in the heat of the moment. Pay attention to your movements, positioning, and decisions. By analyzing your performance, you can make more informed adjustments and become a better player.

Encouraging a **growth mindset** is all about focusing on improvement and learning rather than just winning or losing. Imagine you're playing a game, and your team loses. Instead of feeling defeated, think about what you learned. Maybe you discovered a new strategy or realized you need to work on your speed. A growth mindset means seeing failures as opportunities to grow. It's about celebrating small victories and progress, not just the final outcome. When you approach football with this mindset, every practice and game becomes a chance to learn something new and improve.

Mistakes are a natural part of the learning process. Everyone from beginners to pros makes them. What matters is how you respond. Instead of getting discouraged, see each mistake as a valuable lesson. Listen to feedback from your coaches and teammates—they're there to help you succeed. Use self-analysis tools like game diaries and video reviews to understand your performance better. And most importantly, adopt a growth mindset. Focus on improving and learning rather than just the end result. This approach will help you become a better player and a more resilient person, both on and off the field.

In this chapter, we've explored how football teaches valuable lessons that go beyond the field—teamwork, leadership, sportsmanship, resilience, goal setting, discipline, and learning from mistakes. These skills and values are not just for winning games but for succeeding in life. As we move to the next chapter, get ready to discover how football can be a source of fun, creativity, and joy.

Chapter 6

MAKING FOOTBALL FUN

Imagine this: You're hanging out with your friends, talking about all the cool things you've learned about football. Suddenly, someone throws out a wild fact about a game from years ago, and everyone is amazed. That's the kind of fun we're going to have in this chapter. We're diving into some of the most surprising and interesting football trivia, plus creating quizzes that will test your knowledge and keep you on your toes. Let's make learning about football as exciting as playing it!

6.1 Football Trivia: Fun Facts and Quizzes

Did you know the longest field goal ever made in an NFL game was 66 yards? It was kicked by Justin Tucker of the Baltimore Ravens in 2021. That's more than half the length of a football field! Did you know the Super Bowl as we know it today was first played in January 1967? Or how about this: The highest-scoring game in NFL history was played between the Washington Redskins and the New York Giants in 1966, with a combined score of 113 points. Washington won 72-41. The Washington team is now named the Washington Commanders. These facts show just how incredible and unpredictable football can be, with moments that leave fans in awe and history books filled with unforgettable records.

Football isn't just about the present; it has a rich history filled with legendary players and unforgettable moments. For example, did you know that Jerry Rice, one of the greatest wide receivers of all time, started playing football in college almost by accident? He was discovered by a college coach who saw him playing intramural sports. Rice went on to set records that still stand today like the most career receiving yards with 22,895. Another fun fact: The original Super Bowl trophy, named the Vince Lombardi Trophy, is made by Tiffany & Co. and weighs about seven pounds. It's awarded to the winning team each year, and it's a symbol of hard work and dedication.

Now that you're armed with some cool trivia let's see how much you remember. Quizzes are a fun way to test your knowledge and see what you've learned. Here's a quiz to get you started:

1. What year was the first Super Bowl played?

   - A) 1960
   - B) 1967
   - C) 1972

2. Who holds the record for the most receiving yards in the NFL?

   - A) Tom Brady
   - B) Jerry Rice
   - C) Emmitt Smith

3. How many points is a touchdown worth?

   - A) 3
   - B) 6
   - C) 7

4. What is the name of the trophy awarded to the Super Bowl champions?

- A) Lombardi Trophy
- B) Heisman Trophy
- C) Stanley Cup

Advanced Terms

Here are a few more terms we haven't gone over. You can challenge your friends and family to see who knows more football terms. Turn it into a friendly competition, and see who can become the ultimate football vocabulary champion!

Pick-Six – a defensive players intercepts the ball and runs it back for a TD

Hail Mary – a desperate long pass play usually at the end of a half or game

Red Zone – the last 20 yards before the end zone

Audible – a QB changing the play call at the line of scrimmage right before the snap

Play Action – a play that looks to be a run play but is actually a pass play

Wildcat Formation – a RB or WR lines up in the QB position

> **Answers:** 1B, 2B, 3B, 4A

6.2 What Would You Do? Scenario-Based Questions

Imagine you're the quarterback in a high stakes game. It's fourth down, and your team is just a few yards away from the end zone. The clock is ticking, and the crowd is on the edge of their seats. What play do you call? Do you go for a quick pass to your wide receiver, hoping they can outrun the defense? Or do you hand the ball off to your running back, betting on their ability to break through the defensive line? These kinds of real game scenarios put you in the driver's seat, challenging you to think like a coach and make critical decisions.

Let's break down a few hypothetical situations. Suppose it's fourth down and inches to go. You're on the opponent's 5-yard line, and your team is behind by six points with only 10 seconds left. A pass play might be risky because if it's incomplete, the clock stops, and you lose your chance. On the other hand, a running play could eat up precious time but might be safer to execute. What would you do? Think about the strengths of your players and the weaknesses of the defense. Maybe your running back has been unstoppable all game, making a run the safer bet. Or perhaps your wide receiver has a knack for making clutch catches.

Now, let's consider a scenario beyond the field. Imagine a player on the opposing team has been taunting your teammates all game. You have the ball and can either ignore them and focus on your play or let their words get to you and react. What's the best course of action? This situation isn't just about football skills; it's about sportsmanship and keeping your cool under pressure. Ignoring the taunts and focusing on your game shows maturity and keeps you in control. Reacting might lead to penalties or distract you from your goal.

Ask your friends what they would do in a fourth down situation and why. Maybe they have different insights based on their experiences and understanding of the game. Talking to your coach can provide a deeper understanding of football strategies and help you learn why certain decisions are made. Family members might offer perspectives on sportsmanship and handling pressure, drawing from their own life experiences.

The variety of situations you can explore is endless. Think about a time when you have to decide whether to go for a two-point conversion or kick an extra point. The score is tied, and the game is in its final moments. A two-point conversion could win the game outright, but it's riskier. An extra point might send the game into overtime, giving your team another chance. What would you do? This decision involves understanding the probabilities and weighing the risks and rewards.

Another scenario could involve team dynamics. Imagine you're the team captain, and one of your teammates is feeling down because they missed a crucial tackle. How do you handle this? Do you give them a pep talk, reminding them of their strengths and encouraging them to keep trying? Or do you focus on the next play, hoping they'll shake it off? Supporting your teammates and building their confidence can be just as important as making the right play call. It fosters a positive team environment and helps everyone perform better.

In addition to tactical decisions, consider ethical dilemmas. Suppose you see a teammate break a minor rule during practice, like skipping a drill. Do you call them out or let it slide? Think about the long-term impact on team discipline and integrity. Addressing the issue respectfully can reinforce the importance of following rules and working hard, even when no one is watching.

These scenario based questions are more than just mental exercises. They're opportunities to practice critical thinking, understand football strategies, and develop important life skills. By putting yourself in these hypothetical situations and discussing your choices, you'll gain a deeper appreciation for the complexities of football and the values it teaches. So, what would you do?

6.3 Football in Movies and Books: Pop Culture Fun

Imagine settling down on the couch, popcorn in hand, ready to watch a movie that brings the excitement and drama of football to life. There are some fantastic kid friendly football movies out there that not only capture the thrill of the game but also teach valuable lessons. One must-see is *The Little Giants*, a fun film about an underdog team that shows the power of teamwork and believing in yourself. Another classic is *Remember the Titans*, which tackles themes of friendship and overcoming prejudice, all while showcasing some epic football action. For a more recent pick, *The Game Plan*, starring The Rock, blends humor, heart, and football, making it a great choice for family movie night.

Books can be just as captivating by offering a deep dive into the world of football through engaging stories. *Football Genius* by Tim Green is a great read for young football fans. It tells the story of a kid who can predict football plays before they happen, intertwining mystery and sports in a way that keeps you hooked. Another fantastic book is *Kickoff!* by Tiki and Ronde Barber, based on the real-life experiences of the twin brothers who went on to become NFL stars. This book highlights the importance of hard work and determination. If you're into biographies, *Game Changers: The Story of Venus and Serena Williams* includes a section on their journey in sports, showing how sports fits into a larger world of athletic achievement.

To make these movies and books even more engaging, try discussing them with your friends and family or even in a classroom setting. Here are a few discussion questions to spark some interesting conversations.

For *The Little Giants*, you might ask:
- "What did you learn about teamwork from the movie?"
- "How did the characters overcome their fears?"
For *Remember the Titans*,
- "How did the team learn to work together despite their differences?"
- "What role did the coach play in uniting the team?"

These questions help you think deeper about the themes and lessons in the stories, making the experience more enriching.

And let's not forget about a pop culture quiz! Test your knowledge of football in movies and books with some fun questions. For example:

1. In *The Game Plan*, what is the name of The Rock's character?
    - A) Joe Kingman
    - B) Mike Matthews
    - C) Tom Brady

2. What team do the kids form in *The Little Giants*?
    - A) The Giants
    - B) The Cowboys
    - C) The Bears

3. In *Football Genius*, what unique ability does the main character have?
    - A) Super speed
    - B) The ability to predict plays
    - C) Incredible strength

4. Who are the authors of *Kickoff!*?
    - A) Tim Green and Mike Lupica
    - B) Tiki and Ronde Barber
    - C) Jerry Spinelli and Matt Christopher

These quizzes make learning about football in pop culture fun and interactive. You could even organize a football movie night with your friends or family. Afterwards, each of you take turns writing out questions about the movie to ask the group, creating your own trivia game. It's a great way to share your love of the sport and discover new stories and films.

Football in movies and books offers a unique way to experience the game, blending entertainment with valuable lessons. Whether you're watching a movie, reading a book, or creating your own story, there's always something new to learn and enjoy. So grab a book, start up a movie, and let the magic of football in pop culture inspire and entertain you.

Answers: 1A, 2A, 3B, 4B

6.4 Hosting a Football Themed Party

Imagine this: it's game day, and you're hosting the ultimate football themed party for your family or friends. The excitement is in the air, and everyone is ready to have a blast. Let's plan this step-by-step to make sure your party is a touchdown!

First things first, you need to set the scene with some awesome decorations. Think about creating a football field right in your living room or backyard. Use green tablecloths for the field and white tape to mark the yard lines. You can make goalposts out of PVC pipes or even use yellow pool noodles. Hang up banners with your favorite teams' colors and logos. Do-it-yourself (DIY) decorations can add a personal touch to your party and make it even more special. A fun project is to make table centerpieces using small footballs or helmets filled with snacks or flowers. You can also create a "playbook" for each guest, which includes the schedule of activities, trivia questions, and a space for autographs and messages from friends. These DIY projects not only decorate your space but also engage your guests in the party's theme.

No party is complete without some delicious snacks, and football themed food will be fun to share with your guests. Start with football shaped sandwiches. Simply use a football shaped cookie cutter (or you can use a regular knife, be sure to ask first!) to cut out sandwiches and add your favorite fillings. Try making "football pizza pockets" by filling crescent roll dough with pizza toppings and shaping them like footballs. Use a toothpick to create the laces before baking. Another fun idea is to make "football brownies." Bake a batch of brownies and use a football-shaped cookie cutter to cut them out. Pipe white icing to create the laces on top. For a refreshing treat, make "football punch" by mixing fruit juices and adding sliced fruits. For a healthy option, use a watermelon as a bowl and fill it with a variety of fruits. Don't forget the classic snacks like popcorn, chips, and dip, but serve them in football themed bowls, if you have them. These snacks are not only delicious but also add to the festive atmosphere.

You can also set up mini games like a football toss, where guests can throw a foam football through a hoop or into a target (maybe a small laundry basket). You can also organize a skills challenge with different stations, such as a passing accuracy test or a timed obstacle course that mimics a football drill. For a more relaxed activity, create a football trivia game where players answer questions about the sport. You might decide to have small prizes for the winners, like mini footballs or team stickers.

Imagine enjoying the tasty snacks and having a blast doing the activities you've planned. Hosting a football themed party is all about creating memories and celebrating the sport you love with the people you care about. With a little creativity and planning, your party will be a hit, and everyone will leave with a smile on their face.

So, grab your decorations, whip up some football snacks, and get ready for a day of fun, laughter, and football. Your party is sure to be a touchdown!

Chapter 7

FOOTBALL FOR ALL: DIVERSITY AND INCLUSION

Imagine this: You're watching a football game, and the camera zooms in on a player who just made an amazing play. As the commentator starts talking about his journey, you realize he comes from a background very different from what you expected. Football is a sport where people from all walks of life can shine, and this chapter is all about celebrating that diversity. We're going to explore how football has historically been viewed, challenge some stereotypes, and share awesome stories of players who've broken barriers and inspired millions.

7.1 Breaking Stereotypes: Diverse Backgrounds in Football

For a long time, people had certain stereotypes about football players. You might have heard things like, "Football players are all the same," or "They come from similar backgrounds." But that's far from the truth. Football is played by people from all over the world, with different cultures, races, and backgrounds. Historically, some people thought that only certain kinds of people could excel in football, but real-life stories show us otherwise. Take **Warren Moon**, for example. Warren was a Black quarterback who faced a lot of prejudice early in his career. Many coaches didn't believe a Black player could succeed as a quarterback. But Warren didn't let that stop him. He worked incredibly hard, eventually becoming one of the greatest quarterbacks in both the CFL and NFL and proving that talent and hard work know no color.

Now, some players come from diverse and underrepresented groups but still rocked the football world. One standout is **Hines Ward**. Hines was born to a Korean mother and a Black father. Growing up, he faced bullying and discrimination because of his mixed heritage. But Hines didn't let that keep him down. Instead, he used it as motivation to become one of the toughest wide receivers in NFL history. He played for the Pittsburgh Steelers and helped them win two Super Bowls. His story shows that no matter where you come from, you can achieve greatness. Another inspiring player is Samoan-American **Troy Polamalu**, known for his long, curly hair and fierce playing style. Troy's heritage is deeply important to him, and he's used his platform to bring attention to the Samoan community, showing that football can be a way to celebrate and share your culture.

Football leagues and organizations are also working hard to promote diversity at all levels. For instance, the NFL has the "Rooney Rule," which requires teams to interview minority candidates for head coaching and senior football operation jobs. This rule helps ensure that people of all backgrounds get a fair shot at these important positions. On the amateur level, programs like "Play Like a Girl" and "Girls Flag Football" encourage young girls to play football, breaking the stereotype that football is only for boys. Schools and community leagues are increasingly offering scholarships and grants to kids from low-income families, making sure that everyone has the chance to play. These initiatives are vital because they create opportunities for everyone to get involved in the sport, regardless of their background.

Seeing players from diverse backgrounds succeed in football can be incredibly inspiring. Representation matters because it helps break down barriers and shows that football is truly for everyone. And it's not just about seeing people who look like you. It's also about realizing that football is a sport that welcomes everyone, no matter their race, gender, or socio-economic status. When we see diversity on the field, it encourages everyone to pursue their interests in football and feel like they belong.

> **Reflection Section: What's Your Story?**
> Think about your own background and what makes you unique. Write down three things that you think might be different about you compared to others. Then think about how these differences can be your strengths, just like they were for players like Hines Ward and Troy Polamalu. How can you use your unique story to inspire others and achieve your own goals in football or any other area of your life? This exercise will help you see that your differences are what make you special and that you have the potential to achieve great things, just like the diverse players we've talked about.

Football is more than just a game; it's a platform where people from all walks of life come together, break stereotypes, and inspire others. Whether it's through challenging common perceptions, celebrating the success stories of underrepresented groups, or supporting initiatives that promote diversity, football shows us that everyone has a place on the field. So, as you watch your next game or step onto the field yourself, remember that football is for everyone, and that includes you.

7.2 Accessibility in Sports: Making Football Inclusive

Imagine wanting to play football but being told you can't, either because of a physical disability or because your family can't afford the gear. These are real barriers that many kids face, making it hard to join in on the fun. Physical disabilities can make traditional football challenging. For example, running or catching the ball might be difficult for someone in a wheelchair. Economic barriers also stop kids from playing. Football gear, like helmets, pads, and cleats, can be expensive, and some families can't afford it. These barriers can make kids feel left out, but thankfully, there are ways to break them down and make football accessible to everyone.

There are some incredible programs and technologies designed to help kids overcome these barriers and get out on the field. One awesome example is wheelchair football. This adaptation of the game uses specially designed wheelchairs that allow kids with physical disabilities to play. The rules are modified to suit the players' needs, but the spirit of the game remains the same. Kids get to experience the thrill of scoring a touchdown or making a big play, just like anyone else. Another great initiative is grants and scholarships for underprivileged youth. Organizations like the NFL Foundation and local community programs offer financial assistance for kids who want to play but need help to afford the equipment or fees. These grants ensure that money isn't a barrier to enjoying the game. Some schools and community leagues even provide free equipment rentals, making it easier for everyone to participate.

Let's talk about some inspiring success stories of individuals who have overcome these barriers to succeed in football. Take the story of **Ezra Frech**, a young athlete born with a congenital limb difference. Despite his challenges, Ezra didn't let anything stop him from pursuing his dreams. He became an amazing athlete, participating in multiple sports, including football. Ezra's determination and positive attitude have inspired many, showing that physical disabilities don't have to limit your dreams. Another incredible story is that of **Anthony Robles**, who was born with one leg. Although he became famous as a wrestler, his story is relevant here because it shows the power of perseverance. Anthony didn't let his disability define him; instead, he worked hard and became a champion. His story is a powerful reminder that with the right mindset and support, you can achieve anything.

Community support and inclusive policies play a huge role in making football accessible to all. Local communities can come together to support kids who want to play football. This might include fundraising events to buy equipment, volunteering as coaches, or simply cheering from the sidelines. Schools and sports organizations can adopt inclusive policies that ensure everyone gets a chance to play. For example, some schools have "No Cut" policies, meaning every kid who tries out for the team gets to be a part of it. This approach encourages participation and helps kids build confidence and skills, regardless of their initial ability level. Inclusive policies also mean providing training for coaches to understand and support players with different needs, ensuring that everyone feels welcome and valued.

> **Interactive Exercise: Your Accessibility Action Plan**
> Think about ways you can help make football more accessible in your community. Write down three actions you can take to support kids who face physical or economic barriers. Maybe you can organize a fundraiser at your school, volunteer to help at a local league, or spread the word about grants and scholarships available for underprivileged kids. Creating an action plan will help you realize that you have the power to make a difference and ensure that everyone has the chance to enjoy the game.

Football is a sport that should be accessible to everyone, no matter their physical abilities or financial situation. By addressing the barriers that prevent some kids from playing, supporting programs and technologies that aid accessibility, celebrating success stories of individuals who have overcome challenges, and fostering community support and inclusive policies, we can make football a game for all. Whether it's through raising awareness, volunteering, or simply being a supportive friend, you can make a big difference in someone's life and help them experience the joy of football.

7.3 From All Walks of Life: Unique Football Stories

Imagine discovering that your favorite football player didn't start out dreaming of touchdowns and Super Bowl rings. Some players stumble into football almost by accident, coming from backgrounds that you wouldn't usually associate with the sport. Take **Antonio Gates**, for example. Gates initially pursued basketball and even played at Kent State

University, where he led his team to the Elite Eight. It wasn't until after college that he decided to try out for the NFL. Despite never having played college football, Gates' athleticism and determination earned him a spot with the San Diego Chargers. He went on to become one of the best tight ends in NFL history. His story shows that your path to football can be as unique as you are, and sometimes the skills you develop in other areas can make you an even better player.

Personal backgrounds can have a huge impact on how players approach the game. Think about someone like **Patrick Mahomes**, who grew up with a father who was a professional baseball player. This unique upbringing influenced his playing style, especially his ability to throw the football in ways that seem almost impossible. Mahomes often makes throws that look more like baseball pitches, using sidearm angles and quick releases to get the ball to his receivers. His background in baseball has given him a different perspective on how to play quarterback, making him one of the most exciting and innovative players in the league today. Another great example is wide receiver **Larry Fitzgerald**, who credits his disciplined approach to football to the values instilled in him by his grandfather, a pastor. Fitzgerald's upbringing taught him the importance of hard work, humility, and giving back to the community, which is evident both in his playing style and his off-field actions.

Some players use their platform in football to advocate for social change and community development. **Malcolm Jenkins**, a former safety in the NFL, is well-known not just for his skills on the field but also for his commitment to social justice. Jenkins co-founded the Players Coalition, an organization that focuses on criminal justice reform, education, and economic advancement in underprivileged communities. Through his work, Jenkins has shown that football players can be champions of change, using their influence to make a positive impact on society. Another player who made waves is **Chris Long**, a former defensive end who donated his entire 2017 salary to various educational initiatives. Long's efforts have helped provide scholarships, build schools, and support educational programs across the country. These players remind us that football is not just about what happens on the field; it's also about what you can do off the field to help others and make the world a better place.

The lessons learned from these unique stories can be incredibly motivating. One key lesson is that there's no single path to success. Whether you start out playing another sport like Antonio Gates or grow up in a unique environment like Patrick Mahomes, your background can shape you into a fantastic football player in ways you might not expect. Another important lesson is the value of using your platform for good. Seeing players like Malcolm Jenkins and Chris Long make significant contributions to their communities can inspire you to think about how you can make a difference, no matter what your age or situation. These stories teach us that football is more than just a game; it's a way to learn valuable life skills, inspire others, and make a positive impact.

Think about what makes you unique. Maybe you have a talent in another sport, or perhaps you've grown up in a family that values education and community service. Maybe no one in your family has played football. How can these experiences shape your approach to football or any other passion you have? Write down a few ways you think your background can help you in different areas of your life. This exercise will help you see that your unique journey is a strength, not a limitation and that you can achieve great things by embracing who you are.

Football is a sport that welcomes everyone, no matter where they come from or how they started. Whether you're on the field or off, your experiences and values can shape you into someone who not only excels in the sport but also makes a positive impact on the world around you. So, as you continue your own journey, remember that your unique story is something to be proud of, and it just might be the thing that sets you apart and helps you succeed.

7.4 Charities and Causes Supported by Football Players

Imagine discovering that your favorite football player not only scores touchdowns but also makes a difference off the field. Many players start charities and foundations to support causes close to their hearts, showing that being a hero isn't just about what you do on the field. For example, **J.J. Watt** (T.J. Watt's older brother), a defensive end known for his incredible strength and plays, founded the J.J. Watt Foundation. His charity focuses on providing after-school athletic programs for kids, ensuring they have a safe place to play sports and stay active. He also started fundraising efforts after Hurricane Harvey. Watt set out to raise $200,000 for hurricane relief but ended up collecting over $37 million! This money went towards rebuilding homes, schools, and community centers, and helped thousands of families get back on their feet. Then there's the **Peyton Manning** Children's Hospital, a project dear to the legendary quarterback. Manning's foundation provides top-notch medical care for children, making sure they get the treatment they need, regardless of their family's financial situation. Thanks to the hospital's care, funded in part by Manning's foundation, a young boy named Alex received life-saving surgery. Alex made a full recovery and now enjoys playing sports just like any other kid.

Another standout initiative is the 15 and the Mahomies Foundation. **Patrick Mahomes**, the dynamic quarterback for the Kansas City Chiefs, started this foundation to improve the lives of children through health, wellness, and education programs. His foundation supports various projects, like building playgrounds and funding educational scholarships. Then there's the **Larry Fitzgerald** First Down Fund, which helps kids and families in crisis, providing support for health and education. Fitzgerald's foundation organizes football camps for kids, offers school supplies, and even helps with medical expenses for families in need. These foundations show how football players use their fame and resources to help others, creating lasting impacts in their communities.

> The impact of these charities can be seen in the lives they touch. These stories show how the generosity of football players can create real, positive changes, proving that their influence goes far beyond the gridiron.

If you're wondering how you and your family can get involved and support these great causes, there are plenty of ways to contribute. Donations are always welcome; even small amounts can make a big difference. Besides donating money, you can also volunteer your time. Many foundations organize events like charity runs, football camps, and community cleanups where volunteers are needed. Participating in these events is a great way to help and meet new people who share your passion for giving back. Another fun way to contribute is by participating in charity events. For example, the 15 and the Mahomies Foundation often hosts fundraising events where you can join in the activities, meet other supporters, and even get a chance to see Patrick Mahomes in action!

Learning about philanthropy and the importance of giving back is something that can start at any age. Philanthropy is a big word that means helping others and making the world a better place. Even as a young person, there are ways you can make a difference. Think about what you're passionate about. Is it helping other kids, protecting animals, or keeping the environment clean? Once you know what you care about, you can find ways to help. Maybe you can organize a small fundraiser at your school, like a bake sale or a car wash, and donate the money to a cause you care about. You can also spread the word about these charities. Talk to your friends and family about the fantastic work these foundations do and encourage them to get involved too. The more people know about these causes, the more support they can get, which means they can help even more people.

Think about how you can make a difference in your own community. Are there local charities or organizations that need help? Maybe there's a food bank that needs volunteers or a park that could use some cleaning up.

You can talk to your parents, teachers, or community leaders about how you can get involved. Remember, making a difference doesn't always require much time or money. Sometimes, just being kind and helping out where you can make a huge impact. By learning about the importance of philanthropy and taking action, you can be a role model just like your favorite football players.

Football players show us that true greatness comes from what you do on and off the field. Their foundations and charitable work make a real difference in the world, helping those in need and inspiring others to do the same. Whether it's through donations, volunteering, or simply spreading the word, you and your family can be part of this positive change. So, think about how you can contribute, start small, and remember that every little bit helps. Your efforts can make a big difference in someone's life, just like the great football players we admire.

7.5 The Role of Fans: Supporting Your Local Team

Imagine the excitement of cheering for your local high school football team under the bright Friday night lights. Being a fan is about more than just watching games; it's about showing your support in meaningful ways that can lift your team higher. One great way to support your local team is by attending their games. Your presence in the stands, cheering loudly and waving a banner, can boost the players' morale and energize them. But there are other ways to show your support. You can volunteer to help at team events, like organizing fundraisers or helping set up for games. Maybe you're good at art, so make some colorful posters to hang around school or the community to get everyone excited about the next game. Even small gestures can mean a lot.

Supporting your local football team can create a strong sense of community identity and pride. When everyone comes together to cheer for the home team, it creates a bond that goes beyond the game. It's like being part of a big family where everyone shares the same goal. This shared experience can bring people closer, turning neighbors into friends.

Think about the pride you feel when your team wins a big game. It's a feeling everyone in the community shares, making you all feel connected. Local businesses often get involved, sponsoring teams or hosting events to celebrate victories. This kind of support strengthens the community, making it a place where everyone feels they belong.

Being a responsible fan is just as important as being a passionate one. Good sportsmanship and respectful behavior set a positive example for everyone around you. Cheering loudly for your team is great, but it's also important to respect the opposing team and their fans. Avoid negative chants or booing; instead, focus on encouraging your team. If a player from the other team makes a great play, it's okay to applaud their effort. This kind of positive behavior reflects well on your community and shows that you value the spirit of the game. Remember, how you act as a fan can influence others, especially younger kids who look up to you. Being a respectful and supportive fan, you help create a welcoming and enjoyable atmosphere for everyone.

There are so many fun and creative ways to show team spirit and get everyone excited about the game. Wearing team colors on game day is a simple way to show your support. You can also participate in team spirit activities, like pep rallies or community parades. These events are a blast and give you a chance to show your enthusiasm while celebrating with others. If you're feeling extra creative, why not start a fan club at your school? You can plan activities, make signs, and get more people involved in supporting your team. The more spirit and excitement you bring, the more fun everyone will have, and the more your team will feel your support.

Supporting your local football team is about more than just showing up to games. It's about being part of a community, showing respect, and spreading enthusiasm. By getting involved in different ways, you can help create a positive and supportive environment that lifts your team and strengthens your community. Whether through creative activities, responsible behavior, or simply cheering your heart out, your support matters and can have a big impact on your team and your community.

Chapter 8

BEYOND THE GAME

Imagine you're on the football field, the stadium lights are beaming down, and the crowd is cheering wildly. You feel that adrenaline rush, that focus, that drive to do your very best. Now picture taking that same energy and applying it to your schoolwork. Sounds a bit crazy maybe, but you can do it! In this chapter, we're going to explore how the skills and lessons you learn on the football field can help you excel in the classroom. Because guess what? Being a football player isn't just about scoring touchdowns; it's about becoming a well-rounded, disciplined, and focused individual.

8.1 From the Field to the Classroom: Applying Football Discipline to Academics

One of the most important skills you learn in football is discipline. Think about it: every practice, every drill, every game requires you to be on your A-game. This same discipline can be a game-changer when it comes to your schoolwork. Just like you have a practice schedule, you can create a homework schedule. Set specific times for studying and stick to them, just like you would for football practice. Time management is essential. In football, you have to manage the clock and know when to speed up the play or take a timeout. Similarly, in school you need to balance your time between different subjects and projects and even take breaks to recharge.

Another skill from football that's incredibly useful in school is strategic planning. In football, you don't just run around hoping to score; you follow a playbook. You have a strategy. The same goes for studying. Break down your homework into manageable tasks. If you have a big project, plan out what you need to do each day to complete it on time. This way, you're not rushing at the last minute, just like you wouldn't run a last-minute, unplanned play in a game. Strategic planning helps you stay organized and reduces stress, making it easier to tackle big assignments.

Let's talk about focus and concentration. In football, you need to focus before every play. We've talked about taking deep breaths, visualizing the play, or even giving a quick pep talk to yourself to succeed on the field. This mental focusing can also be super helpful in school. Before starting a test or a complex project, take a moment to clear your mind. Visualize yourself doing well. This can help you stay calm and focused. Techniques like deep breathing or positive self-talk can improve your concentration at school, just as they do on the field. It's like having your own mental playbook for staying sharp and ready.

Setting academic goals is another area where football skills come in handy. Just like in football, you can use the SMART goal method for your classes. Make your goals Specific, Measurable, Achievable, Relevant, and Time-bound. For example, instead of saying, "I want to do better in math," you could say, "I want to improve my math grade from a B to an A by the end of the semester by studying for 30 minutes each day." Breaking down your goals into smaller, specific steps can make them easier to achieve, just like breaking down a football game into individual plays.

Handling pressure is something every football player knows well. Whether it's the final seconds of a game or a crucial play, you learn to cope with stress. These strategies can also help you in school. When facing a big test or presentation, use the same techniques you use on the field. Take deep breaths, visualize success, and remind yourself that you've prepared for this. Sometimes, breaking the task into smaller parts can make it seem less overwhelming. For instance, if you have a big test, break your study sessions into 20-minute chunks with short breaks in between. This makes studying more manageable and less stressful.

These skills—discipline, time management, strategic planning, focus, goal setting, and handling pressure—aren't just for football; they're for life. They can help you become a better student, a better athlete, and a better person overall. So next time you're on the field, remember that everything you're learning can help you off the field, too. Football is more than a game; it's a way to develop skills that will benefit you in all areas of your life.

Make your goals:
– **S**mart
– **M**easurable
– **A**chievable
– **R**elevant
– **T**ime-bound

Interactive Exercise: Your Academic Playbook

Just like a football playbook, create an academic playbook for yourself. Write down your weekly schedule, including study times, homework deadlines, and important dates. Set at least one academic goal using the SMART method. For example:

Goal: Improve my science grade from a B to an A by the end of the semester.

– **S**pecific: Study science for 30 minutes every day.
– **M**easurable: Track my quiz and test scores to see improvement.
– **A**chievable: Focus on one chapter each week.
– **R**elevant: Science is important for understanding the world and doing well in school.
– **T**ime-bound: Achieve this by the end of the semester.

Having your academic playbook will help you stay organized and focused, just like a real football playbook helps you succeed on the field. So grab a notebook and start planning!

8.2 Leadership Skills on and off the Field

Imagine you're on a football team, and it's a tough game. The captain steps up, not just by shouting orders or making big plays, but through qualities everyone respects and follows. Great football captains are known for their integrity, communication, and empathy. Integrity means doing the right thing, even when no one is watching. It's about being honest and fair, whether you're on the field or in the classroom. When you show integrity, people trust you more, and a team with trust is a team that works well together. Communication is another big one. A good leader talks and listens. They make sure everyone knows the plan and feels heard. This skill is super helpful in group projects at school, too. And then there's empathy—understanding and sharing the feelings of others. Empathy helps you connect with your teammates, friends, and family, making you someone people feel comfortable turning to.

Leading by example is one of the most powerful ways to show leadership. Think about it: when you see someone working hard and staying positive, it inspires you to do the same. On the football field, this might mean giving your all during practice, encouraging your teammates, and staying focused during the game. Off the field, you can lead by example in group projects at school or during family activities. If you're working on a school project, take the initiative to start the research or offer to be the one who compiles everyone's work. When you show responsibility and dedication, others will follow suit. At home, it might mean helping out with chores without being asked or being the one to suggest a fun family activity. Leading by example shows that actions speak louder than words.

Managing a sports team isn't just about calling plays; it's about learning how to manage groups and projects. One of the key lessons in team management is delegation. This means knowing when to do something yourself and when to let someone else handle it. In football, a quarterback can't do everything—they need to trust their receivers, linemen, and running backs to do their jobs. The same goes for managing a school project. Maybe you're great at writing, but your friend is awesome at making presentations. By delegating tasks based on everyone's strengths, the whole team can perform better. Trust is a huge part of this. Just like in football, where you trust your teammate to catch the ball, you need to trust your classmates or family members to do their part. This trust builds a stronger, more cohesive team.

Conflicts are bound to happen, whether you're on a football team or working on a group project. How you handle these conflicts can make a big difference. In football, conflicts might arise over play choices or during intense moments in the game. Great leaders know how to address these issues calmly and fairly. They listen to both sides, find common ground, and work towards a solution that benefits the team. For example, if two players are arguing about who should start in a game, a good leader might remind them that the team's success is more important than individual roles. In school, conflicts can happen over differences in opinions or who does what in a project. The same approach—listening, finding common ground, and focusing on the group's goal—can help resolve these conflicts effectively. By handling conflicts well, you contribute to a positive and productive environment, whether it's on the field, in the classroom, or at home.

Leadership skills learned on the football field are incredibly valuable in everyday life. Being a good leader means having integrity, communicating well, and showing empathy. Leading by example inspires others and shows that actions matter. Managing a team teaches you about delegation and trust while handling conflicts effectively helps maintain a positive environment. These skills make you a better teammate, student, and family member. So the next time you're playing football, remember that you're not just learning how to score touchdowns or make tackles—you're also learning how to be a leader in every aspect of your life.

8.3 Football and Community Service: Giving Back

Giving back through football can have a big impact on your personal growth. When you volunteer or participate in community service, you develop empathy and a broader perspective on life. You start to see the world through other people's eyes and understand the challenges they face. This can make you more compassionate and understanding, qualities that are valuable both on and off the field. Plus, helping others can make you feel good inside, boosting your confidence and self-esteem. It's amazing how much you can grow as a person just by giving a little bit of your time and energy to help others.

Involvement in community service also helps you build networks of people you know and foster relationships that might be valuable in the future. When you volunteer, you meet people from all walks of life, including coaches, community leaders, and other volunteers. These connections can open doors to new opportunities, whether it's a recommendation for a college application, a job offer, or simply a new friendship. In this way, networking teaches you the importance of building relationships based on mutual respect and shared goals. It's like creating a team off the field, where everyone works together to make a positive impact.

Imagine organizing a community event where you invite local younger kids to participate in a football clinic. You could recruit your friends and teammates to help run drills and teach basic skills. Not only would you be giving kids a fun and educational experience, but you'd also be practicing leadership and teamwork. You'd be creating a sense of community and showing that football is more than just a game—it's a way to bring people together. These kinds of experiences can be incredibly rewarding and provide valuable lessons that will stay with you for a lifetime.

Engaging in community service through football activities can also teach you important life skills. For example, planning and organizing an event requires you to think ahead, communicate effectively, and manage your time well. These are skills that will serve you well in school, work, and other areas of your life. Plus, they help you become a more responsible and dependable person. It's all about taking the lessons you learn on the field and applying them to real-world situations, making you a more well-rounded person.

Football players often use their platform to support important causes and raise awareness about issues that matter to them. You can do the same by getting involved in community service. Whether it's raising money for a local charity or spreading the word about a cause you care about, you have the power to make a difference. And when others see you taking action, they might be inspired to get involved too. It's all about creating a ripple effect, where one good deed leads to another, and together, we can make the world a better place.

So, next time you think about football, remember it's not just about the touchdowns and tackles. It's about the impact you can make off the field as well. By engaging in community service, you can use your love for the game to help others, grow as a person, and build valuable connections. It's a reminder that football is more than just a sport—it's a way to give back, inspire others, and make a positive difference in the world.

8.4 Future Careers in Football Beyond Playing

Imagine being part of the football world, even if you're not on the field scoring touchdowns or making tackles. There are many exciting career paths in the football world beyond being a player. Think about coaching, where you can guide and inspire the next generation of players, sharing your knowledge and passion for the game. You could become a sports manager, handling everything from team logistics to player contracts and ensuring the team runs smoothly. If you love the business side of things, sports marketing might be for you; you can help promote teams, players, and events, making sure fans stay engaged and excited. And for those who love writing and storytelling, sports journalism offers the chance to cover games, interview players, and bring the excitement of football to life through words.

To pursue these careers, you'll need a mix of education and skills. For coaching, a background in physical education or sports science can be very helpful. Understanding the mechanics of the game, training techniques, and player psychology is crucial. Sports management often requires knowledge in business administration, finance, and law. Courses in these subjects can teach you how to handle contracts, manage budgets, and navigate the legal aspects of sports. If you're interested in sports marketing, studying marketing, communications, or public relations can provide the tools you need to create engaging campaigns and connect with fans. And for sports journalism, a degree in journalism or communications is often required, along with strong writing skills and a passion for storytelling. Interests in subjects like business, communications, or even science can lead to fulfilling careers in the football world.

Gaining experience through internships or volunteering is a fantastic way to get a practical understanding of these careers and open up opportunities. Interning with a local football team, sports organization, or media outlet can give you hands-on experience and a behind-the-scenes look at how things work. You might assist with coaching clinics, help organize events, or even shadow a sports journalist to learn the ropes. Volunteering at community sports programs or charity events hosted by football teams can also provide valuable experience. Plus, it shows your dedication and willingness to work hard, which can impress future employers. These experiences not only teach you the ins and outs of the industry but also help you build a group of contacts who can support and guide you in your career. This is called networking.

Networking is super important in the sports community. Building relationships with coaches, players, sports managers, and other professionals can open doors to new opportunities. Attending football games, sports conferences, and community events where you can meet people in the industry is a great start. Don't be afraid to introduce yourself, ask questions, and show your enthusiasm for football. Joining sports clubs or organizations at school can also help you connect with others who share your interests. These connections can lead to internships, job offers, and valuable advice as you figure out what you want to do when you're older. Remember, the relationships you build today can help you succeed in the future.

The world of football offers so many career paths beyond playing on the field. Whether you're interested in coaching, sports management, sports marketing, or sports journalism, there are endless possibilities to explore. With the right education, skills, experience, and networking, you can turn your passion for football into a fulfilling career. So, dream big, work hard, and remember that the relationships you build along the way can help you achieve your goals. The football industry is filled with opportunities, and with dedication and perseverance, you can find your place in this exciting world.

8.5 Football and Education: Learning Beyond the Field

Imagine you're playing a football game, and you score the winning touchdown. The crowd goes wild, and you feel like you're on top of the world. Now, imagine that same feeling of accomplishment but in the classroom. Excelling in football can open doors to incredible educational opportunities, like scholarships. Colleges often offer scholarships to talented athletes to help pay for their education. These scholarships aren't just about your skills on the field; they also recognize your hard work, dedication, and potential. Think of it as a way to get a great education while continuing to play the sport you love. Winning a scholarship can be a game-changer, allowing you to focus on your studies without worrying about the financial burden of college.

Football isn't just about physical skills; it's also a fantastic teaching tool for various academic subjects. Take physics, for example. When you throw a football, the trajectory or path it follows depends on forces like gravity and air resistance. Understanding these concepts can make you better at judging your throws and catches. Similarly, math plays a big role in football. Keeping track of scores, calculating player stats, and even figuring out the best angles for a play all involve math. For instance, if you're a quarterback, knowing the right angle to throw the ball can mean the difference between a completed pass and an interception. By connecting what you learn in football to your school subjects, you can see how math and science come to life in real-world situations.

Several programs successfully combine football training with academic tutoring, showing that you can excel both on the field and in the classroom. Programs like the NFL's Youth Education Towns (YET) provide after-school tutoring and football training, helping kids improve their grades while developing their athletic skills. These programs often include mentorship from players and coaches, who share their experiences and offer guidance. Being part of such a program can boost your confidence, improve your academic performance, and help you stay focused on your goals. It's like having a support team to help you succeed in every aspect of your life. These programs prove that with the right balance, you can be a star both in sports and academics.

Football also teaches valuable life skills that go beyond the field. For example, planning and strategic thinking are crucial in football. You need to plan your plays, think ahead, and adjust your strategies based on the game situation. These skills are equally important in school and your future career. When you plan a project or a study schedule, you're using the same skills you use to plan a game winning play. Strategic thinking helps you solve problems, make decisions, and stay organized. Execution is another critical skill. In football, it's not just about having a good plan; it's about carrying it out effectively. The same goes for school and work. Whether it's completing a homework assignment or working on a group project, being able to execute your plans well is essential for success.

These experiences prepare you for leadership roles in other areas of your life, like school clubs or future jobs. Football teaches you how to work as part of a team, communicate effectively, and motivate others. These are all skills that will serve you well in any career path you choose. By learning these life skills through football, you're setting yourself up for success in all areas of your life.

Football's benefits extend far beyond the field. Excelling in the sport can provide educational scholarships, opening doors to higher education. Football can also serve as a teaching tool, helping you understand academic subjects like physics and math in a practical and engaging way. Programs that combine football training with academic tutoring show that you can succeed both in sports and school. Finally, the life skills you gain from football, such as planning, strategic thinking, and execution, are invaluable for your educational and career success. As you continue your journey in football, remember that the lessons you learn on the field can help you achieve your dreams off the field as well.

So, as you lace up your cleats and step onto the field, know that you're not just playing a game—you're building a foundation for a bright future. Football is more than a sport; it's a way to learn, grow, and prepare for whatever challenges come your way. Keep pushing, keep learning, and keep striving for greatness in everything you do. The skills and lessons you gain from football will help you succeed in all areas of your life, both now and in the future.

Conclusion

Hey there, young athlete!

Wow, what a journey we've had together! From diving into the basics of football to exploring the incredible stories of legendary players and unsung heroes, we've covered so much ground. Remember, the core mission of this book has always been to inspire, entertain, and educate you through the amazing sport of American football.

We've seen how football isn't just about touchdowns, tackles, and field goals. It's a powerful way to learn life skills, boost your confidence, and become a role model both on and off the field. Through stories, fun quizzes, and interesting trivia, we've explored how football can teach you about teamwork, leadership, and resilience. It's all about showing you how the lessons learned on the field can be applied to everyday life.

One of the most important messages in this book is that football is for everyone. No matter your background, gender, or experience level, you have a place in this sport. We've celebrated the achievements of legendary players, highlighted the journeys of trailblazing female athletes, and shared the inspiring stories of those who broke barriers and defied expectations. Football is a community where everyone can shine, and we hope you've felt that inclusivity and diversity throughout our chapters.

Football is more than just a game; it's a way to grow as a person. It teaches you valuable life lessons like discipline, strategic thinking, and the importance of hard work. It encourages you to stay physically fit, build character, and develop resilience. We've talked about how these skills not only make you a better player but also a better student, friend, and leader. Whether you're planning a game winning play or setting goals for school, the lessons learned from football will guide you in all areas of your life.

We've also stressed the significance of health, safety, and mental well-being. Remember those tips on nutrition and hydration? They're just as important as learning how to throw the perfect pass or make a crucial tackle. Taking care of your body and mind is key to performing your best. Injury prevention and maintaining a positive mindset are essential for your overall well-being. Always listen to your body, prioritize rest and recovery, and keep a balanced approach to training and playing.

Our vision has always been to inspire you to love football and apply the life lessons you've learned to your own everyday life. We want you to be role models and leaders in your communities. Whether it's through football or other passions, strive to be someone who makes a positive impact. Remember, being a leader isn't just about being the best player; it's about inspiring and uplifting those around you.

As you move forward, carry the spirit of football with you. Be a lifelong learner, always eager to grow and improve. Keep striving for excellence, both on and off the field. Embrace leadership roles in your teams and communities. The values and skills you've gained from football will serve you well in every aspect of your life.

I'll leave you with a powerful quote from one of the greatest football figures, Vince Lombardi:

> "It's not whether you get knocked down, it's whether you get up ."

Thank you for joining me on this incredible journey. Your enthusiasm and dedication have made this experience truly special. Keep the spirit of the game alive in your heart and actions. Remember, you have the power to inspire others and make a difference. Keep pushing, keep learning, and keep shining. The world is waiting for you to make your mark.

Let's go!

Keeping the Game Alive

Now that you've made it through *Football for Kids Ages 8-12*, you've got everything you need to dive into the world of football. But don't stop there! One of the best things you can do next is to pass on what you've learned and help other kids find the same excitement.

By leaving your honest review of this book, you're helping others discover all the tips, stories, and fun that come with learning about football. Just like a good pass on the field, sharing your thoughts can keep the love of the game going strong.

Every review makes a difference. It shows future readers where to find the info they're looking for and helps grow a community of kids who love football just like you..

Simply scan the QR code or visit the link below and leave a review:

https://www.amazon.com/review/review-your-purchases/?asin=B0DV5DQ6BC

Thank you for helping spread the love of football.

REFERENCES

Barklund.org. (n.d.). *The basics of football*. https://barklund.org/the-basics-of-football-22/

Sportsbookbonus.com. (n.d.). *Sportsbooks for Atlanta Falcons: How to make money on Atlanta Falcons*. https://www.sportsbookbonus.com/sports/football/nfl/nfc/nfc-south/atlanta-falcons.html

Fit On. (n.d.). *Conquer your sport: Sports-specific workouts*. https://fit-on.net/conquer-your-sport-sports-specific-workouts/

Metro League. (n.d.). *Unveiling the football 4-3 defense: A comprehensive guide*. https://www.metroleague.org/football-4-3-defense_af/

Blognez.com. (n.d.). *The importance of sports in developing conflict resolution skills*. https://blognez.com/the-importance-of-sports-in-developing-conflict-resolution-skills/

Rules of Sport. (n.d.). *American football rules*. https://www.rulesofsport.com/sports/american-football.html

Lifeopedia.com. (n.d.). *Six tips for teaching sports to kids*. https://www.lifeopedia.com/how-to-teach-children-a-sport/

Bleacher Report. (n.d.). *The NFL's greatest role models*. https://bleacherreport.com/articles/714743-the-greatest-role-models-in-nfl-history

Fuel Up to Play 60. (n.d.). *NFL Flag Football curriculum*. https://www.fuelup.org/getmedia/224fb843-2c93-459b-9251-416a4be71099/NFL-Flag-Football-Curriculum.pdf

Clear, J. (n.d.). *The deliberate practice and training of Jerry Rice*. https://jamesclear.com/jerry-rice#:~:text=Most%20remarkable%20were%20his%20six,did%20equally%20strenuous%20weight%20training.

Yardbarker. (2023). *Kurt Warner: Career retrospective*. https://www.yardbarker.com/nfl/articles/kurt_warner_career_retrospective_100423/s1__38062976

NCAA. (2020). *Sarah Fuller makes history as first female to score in a major conference football game*. https://www.ncaa.com/news/football/article/2020-12-12/sarah-fuller-makes-history-first-female-score-major-conference-football-game

New York Times. (n.d.). *Doug Flutie's 'Hail Mary' pass*. https://www.nytimes.com/packages/html/sports/year_in_sports/11.23.html?scp=2&sq=king%20crimson&st=cse

Mojo Sport. (n.d.). *10 fun flag football passing drills*. https://mojo.sport/coachs-corner/10-fun-flag-football-passing-drills/

OT Mom Learning Activities. (n.d.). *Hand-eye coordination activities for kids*. https://www.ot-mom-learning-activities.com/hand-eye-coordination.html

Youth Football Online. (n.d.). *How to tackle with proper tackling technique in youth football*. https://youthfootballonline.com/how-to-tackle-with-proper-tackling-technique-in-youth-football/#:~:text=Summary%3A%20Approach%20the%20ball%20carrier,cloth%20and%20finish%20the%20tackle.

Viqtory Sports. (n.d.). *The complete beginners guide to American football*. https://www.viqtorysports.com/how-to-understand-american-football-beginners-guide/

National Center for Biotechnology Information. (2013). *Sport nutrition for young athletes*. https://www.ncbi.nlm.nih.gov/pmc/articles/PMC3805623/

UW Medicine. (n.d.). *Strengthening mental health for young athletes*. https://give.uwmedicine.org/stories/strengthening-mental-health-for-youth-athletes/

REFERENCES 113

MidAmerica Orthopedics. (n.d.). *Youth football injuries: How to prevent and prepare*. https://midamericaortho.com/blog/371-youth-football-injuries-how-to-prevent-and-prepare

Swimming World Magazine. (n.d.). *7 helpful time management tips for student-athletes*. https://www.swimmingworldmagazine.com/news/7-helpful-time-management-tips-for-student-athletes/

U.S. Department of Health and Human Services. (2020). *Benefits of youth sports*. https://health.gov/sites/default/files/2020-09/YSS_Report_OnePager_2020-08-31_web.pdf

TrueSport. (n.d.). *How to use youth sports to develop strong leaders*. https://truesport.org/leadership/youth-sports-develop-strong-leaders/

Bleacher Report. (n.d.). *10 recent awesome acts of sportsmanship*. https://bleacherreport.com/articles/2635422-10-recent-awesome-acts-of-sportsmanship

Rutgers University. (n.d.). *Goal setting for youth sports*. https://youthsports.rutgers.edu/articles/goal-setting-for-youth-sports/

Science Kids. (n.d.). *Fun American football facts for kids*. https://www.sciencekids.co.nz/sciencefacts/sports/americanfootball.html

Forms.app. (n.d.). *Free online football trivia quiz template*. https://forms.app/en/templates/football-trivia-quiz

Crafting Jeannie. (n.d.). *Football Father's Day pop-up card (Free template)*. https://www.craftingjeannie.com/football-popup-fathers-day/

ABCya. (n.d.). *Sports learning games*. https://www.abcya.com/games/category/sports

Forbes. (2023). *The benefits of youth sports in local communities (And how businesses can support them)*. https://www.forbes.com/sites/forbesbusinesscouncil/2023/06/27/the-benefits-of-youth-sports-in-local-communities-and-how-businesses-can-support-them/

Givelify. (n.d.). *Celebrating four of the most generous football players*. https://www.givelify.com/blog/most-generous-football-players/

TicketSource. (n.d.). *How to plan and organize a sports event in 14 steps*. https://www.ticketsource.us/blog/how-to-plan-a-sport-event

YMCA. (n.d.). *4 benefits of being a volunteer youth sports coach*. https://gwrymca.org/blog/4-benefits-being-volunteer-youth-sports-coach

International Federation of American Football. (n.d.). *International Federation of American Football*. https://www.americanfootball.sport/

Yellowbrick. (n.d.). *The impact of technology on sports performance*. https://www.yellowbrick.co/blog/sports/the-impact-of-technology-on-sports-performance

Sports for AA. (n.d.). *Overcoming challenges: Inspirational stories from young athletes*. https://www.sportsforaa.org/blogs/overcoming-challenges-inspirational-stories-from-young-athletes/

Active Kids. (n.d.). *8 benefits for kids who play football*. https://www.activekids.com/parenting-and-family/articles/8-benef

Made in the USA
Las Vegas, NV
08 May 2025

aa9cfa7d-3cd2-4d18-bc89-16f23d7893ebR01